A SEASON
ON THE MED

A SEASON
ON THE MED

RIVIERA FOOTBALL IN ITALY AND FRANCE
(WITH A TRIP TO ATHENS FOR STAN)

ALEX WADE

First published by Pitch Publishing, 2022

Pitch Publishing
9 Donnington Park,
85 Birdham Road,
Chichester,
West Sussex,
PO20 7AJ
www.pitchpublishing.co.uk
info@pitchpublishing.co.uk

ISBN 978 1 80150 197 2

Typesetting and origination by Pitch Publishing
Printed and bound in Great Britain by TJ Books, Padstow

Contents

By the same author

Non-fiction
Wrecking Machine (2005)
Surf Nation (2007)
Amazing Surfing Stories (2012)

Fiction
Flack's Last Shift (2016)

For Caroline and Maud

Introduction

Swimming Into Stan

SANREMO, ITALY, 6 October 2021. It's a glorious, warm and cloudless day, the kind served up almost daily along the Italian and French Rivieras like a taunt. Homesick? Missing your known life in England? Think again. It's better here. Way, way better.

I'm gently baking in the Wednesday afternoon sun in Stadio Comunale's south-facing stand. Before me, on the kempt grass, the home side, Società Sportiva Dilettantistica Sanremese Calcio or, rather more succinctly, Sanremese, are taking on Piedmont-based Casale. Once an illustrious force in Italian football, rubbing shoulders 100 years ago with leviathans such as Juventus, Genoa, Torino and Milan and winning the national title in the 1913/14 season, now Casale ply their trade in Serie D. Sanremese, their Ligurian opponents, have flirted with Serie B, the second tier of Italian football – once finishing ninth – but for the most part have played in Serie C and Serie D. Their 21st-century history is dominated by serious financial problems, leading to bankruptcy in 2011, but, as seems often the way in Italian football, also reincarnation (for them, in 2015).

This season, stability over the past few years has prompted talk of a return to Serie C.

Before arriving at the ground, I saw four or five surfers in the line-up at the eastern end of Sanremo's beach. The waves were chest-to-shoulder high. The sight made me smile. *There's even surf here*, I thought, as I made my way to the Stadio Comunale. *And what a day to be surfing.*

John agreed. An English expat who, like me, lived just under an hour's drive away in France, John was taken by the surfers, but more so by the simple fact that here, on an early October day, we were set to watch a football match wearing shorts and T-shirts under the endlessly bright Mediterranean sun, in a temperature of around 25°C. 'Look at this! This is the life, Alex, this is the life,' he said.

I wasn't about to argue. I was in love with the Mediterranean – had been for years. Now I lived here. And I loved football. How lucky were we, to be whiling away a Wednesday afternoon in Sanremo, the city of flowers on the Riviera dei Fiori, watching Sanremese v Casale?

* * *

Each day, I swim.

When I swim, I rarely think. I just swim, front crawl, for a mile or thereabouts, here in the Mediterranean Sea. It's immersive, cathartic, regenerative. I emerge having thought about nothing – nothing at all, save whether I might meet a *meduse* – and when I leave the sea, for a few minutes at least, it's as if I could be any age, in any place, with any kind of life ahead or behind me.

But on one swim, in summer 2021 in the middle of the delayed Euro 2020 football championship, I had not just one but two thoughts. They ebbed and flowed as I swam from the *plage pour les chiens* in Garavan, Menton to the rocks outlying Balzi Rossi, a tiny beach over the border from France in Italy.

The first thought was this: Stan Bowles, my idol, played football on the Med.

Stan appeared early in the swim. He wasn't an unwelcome guest. Bowles, arguably the greatest of Queens Park Rangers' many great number tens, had an influence on my life so profound that, when I once had the chance to mention it to him, meant I was taken aback when he replied with his stock-in-trade, deadpan indifference.

'It's such an honour to talk to you,' I said. 'You were my hero as a kid. I spent hours trying to do what you could do with a ball. I just wanted to be you.'

'That's nice,' said Stan.

On that swim, something made my mind conjure up Stan Bowles. A man who took everything in his stride, a man who seemed so nonchalant you could imagine him ambling amiably amid an earthquake, wondering what all the fuss was about. A man who was one of football's magicians and who, on 16 March 1977, was part of the QPR side that lost 3-0 to AEK Athens in the second leg of the UEFA Cup quarter-finals. QPR had beaten AEK 3-0 in the first leg, played in front of a crowd of 23,039 on 2 March at Loftus Road, their Shepherd's Bush home, and so the tie would be settled by penalties at AEK's Nikos Goumas stadium. AEK won 7-6. Needless to say, Bowles converted one of QPR's penalties, and to this day he remains, with Alan Shearer, the joint-highest scoring Englishman in the UEFA Cup (including its present-day incarnation as the Europa League). The pair each netted 11 goals.

* * *

With Caroline, I'd been visiting Menton, the last outpost of the Côte d'Azur before Italy, for a few years when we realised a villa was available to rent on Avenue Katherine Mansfield, in the Garavan *quartier*. Unusually for the French Riviera, it was affordable, but we had a perfectly nice life in Penzance, Cornwall. Should we leave our friends and families? Should we take the plunge? If we did, our daughter, then three, would learn French. That seemed a good thing. Perhaps, as Brexit loomed, it was even a gentle gesture of defiant Europhilia. And what's not to like about the French Riviera, and, especially, Menton?

We'd come to love the town whose name, in French, means 'chin' (though there is no known link between place and name). Its subtropical microclimate is touted as the best in France, but as befits a town belonging, at various times in its history, to the Republic of Genoa, Monaco and Sardinia before becoming part of France in 1860, there's more to Menton than the weather. Its mélange of influences play out in the sounds of the market and the streets, shops and restaurants: you'll hear as much Italian as French, with a smattering of *Mentonasc*, the local dialect. Likewise, the cuisine – regional dishes like *barbajuan* (ravioli) and *pichade* (a sort of onion tart with tomatoes) – owes as much to Italy as to France. There are the luxuriant gardens of Maria Serena, Val-Rahmeh and Serre de la Madone; the medieval Old Town, a labyrinth of narrow streets emanating to and from the basilica Saint

Michel, with houses painted ochre, yellow and pink; the mountains of the Maritime Alps high above. The sea is at every turn and, seemingly everywhere, there is citrus fruit. Fancy an orange? Or a lemon? There are parts of Menton where you can pluck one from a tree.

Menton has it all, and yet is somehow unknown, more a village than a town and, better yet (so far as we were concerned), a world away from the bling and glitz of Monaco, just a few miles to the west.

We'd been visiting long enough to see more than just the sun and the sea. There was a richness to Menton, but a subtlety, too. A poise, a sense of discretion. *Life is good*, said Menton. *But don't rush. Don't exaggerate. Enjoy it.* And for us, it needn't be life, forever. We could stay a while, then see if we wanted to return to the UK or, armed with our *cartes de séjour,* stay put.

There was just one problem: football. Despite being in my 50s, I was still playing twice, sometimes three times, a week in the UK, mostly in Penzance, and if work took me to London, with five- or seven-a-side teams there. When I was in London, I'd faithfully head to the place I'd always known as Loftus Road (it was renamed the Kiyan Prince Foundation Stadium in 2019, in honour of youth player Kiyan Prince, who was stabbed to death in Edgware in May 2006) to see QPR, the club I've supported since childhood. Football – both playing and watching – was fundamental to my life. What would I do in France? There'd be no QPR and I wasn't too hopeful of finding a five-a-side crew after a French friend, based in Menton, expressed consternation at the idea. '*Qu'est-ce que c'est le football à cinq?*' he said, baffled. '*Nous n'avons pas cela ici.*'

'We don't have that here.'

But I was in my 50s. I'd staggered through a few 11-a-side games in my sixth decade but left the field after the last one, when I was 52, so shattered I was now strictly a five- or seven-a-side player only. Even those games, lasting for just an hour, left me battered and creaking for the next 24 hours – if I was lucky. Often enough, a hamstring or calf would pop. I'd rest, return, repeat. Sometimes an old injury would flare up; sometimes I'd pull a muscle I didn't know existed. There was no rhyme or reason to any of this. I could warm up for an hour and still something could go wrong.

For a while (too long, no doubt), I would kid myself that my refusal to quit was admirable, a kind of last stand against the ravages of time. But it was getting silly. Too much hurt, too often. Besides, if I'd long since lost any semblance of mobility, let alone pace, now my touch was starting to let me down. Getting at least a few things right, maybe even scoring a goal or two, was being replaced by pain, miscues and, on one occasion, falling over for no apparent reason.

Don't get me wrong. We're not talking ex-pro standards here. I was only ever an okay Saturday and Sunday league player. But, like thousands – no, millions – around the globe in that category, football still *meant something*. Sometimes I fancied it meant everything. The joy of seeing the net bulge when you score; the satisfaction of a sweet pass and a well-worked move; if Stan Bowles had been your hero, the exquisite thrill of a nutmeg or some other piece of mischief. Beyond that, the camaraderie of the game. If you know football, you can talk to anyone, anywhere in the world, whatever the language or other ostensible barriers between you.

But the mischief was undergoing a shift. Not too kind a one, either. My last stand wasn't just painful physically, it was becoming comedic. Maybe, just maybe, it was time to hang up my boots. In Menton, lapped by the gentle waters of the Mediterranean, I could swap football for swimming. And hey, this is the modern world! I could watch QPR online.

And so, insignificant football-related misgivings shunted to the side, we signed a two-year rental agreement and arrived in Menton on 1 September 2020.

* * *

Life in Menton was everything we hoped for, and more, despite one or two challenges.

In France, if you're opting for state education, the local town hall – *mairie* – determines where your child goes to school. The decision is based on catchment area, and, given we found one cliché, at least, to be true – the French love their red tape – there were hoops to jump through. Brandishing my very rusty and entirely mediocre French A-level, my appointment at the *mairie* went something like this:

'Hello, my name is Alex, and I've just moved here from the UK. I arrived today. And I have an appointment to discuss which school my daughter will attend.'

Cordial response, much checking of computer screens, general conversation among the employees at the mairie tasked with school administration. And then:

'Monsieur Wade, your paperwork is not correct. Please complete these forms and come back tomorrow.'

I did as I was told and, the following day, asked if all was now in order.

'*Oui, bien sur,*' said my new acquaintances, as if there could never have been any doubt. 'Your daughter will go to *maternelle*. The name is École Adrien Camaret.'

This was great, but because we'd arrived the previous day, I felt a couple of weeks to settle in would be a good idea. If we hung out at the beach and had a few leisurely café lunches, our daughter would settle into her new life and maybe even pick up a word or two of French. As it was, at that point she had none.

The good folk at the *mairie* were horrified by this idea. 'Mais non!' they chorused. '*Elle doit commencer lundi!*'

I didn't dare muster a 'vraiment?'. They had fire in their bellies. It was Friday, and our daughter, then three and a half, would be plunged into a new school on Monday.

That same day, Caroline and I visited the *maternelle* – the name for pre-schools in France, attended by three-to six-year-olds. It was halfway up Montée du Souvenir, a steep hill above Menton's Old Town. On the plus side, the location was incredible. Our school run would be along the promenade from Garavan, then disappear into the cobbled streets of Old Town and cross the beautiful mosaic floor which yields the Basilica of Saint-Michel, then take a few more steps and there, at the École Adrien Camaret, our daughter's playtime would have the azure of the Mediterranean, stretching from Menton to Cap Martin, as a backdrop.

The downside. A call to the *maîtresse,* also known as Caroline, revealed that no one at the school spoke any English.

Later that Friday afternoon, while we were swimming at the plage Sablette, a Frenchman reversed his car at speed into the side of the stationary and legitimately parked VW Caravelle we'd driven to France. He hit it with such force that the nearside door, wheel arch and bodywork were crumpled almost beyond repair. An insurance nightmare ensued, with my insurers insisting that getting the vehicle to a garage for repair was my responsibility. They could not recommend a garage, save for one in Germany. They could not organise the recovery of the vehicle to their authorised German garage, or any nearby that I might find. I would have to arrange recovery myself, but if I could do this, I was very welcome to have the VW taken to Germany, where one of their engineers would be delighted to investigate. I was of course welcome to have the vehicle taken to a more convenient garage, too. But whatever I did I would have to do myself. This was a premium 'Serenity for Brits Abroad', total-peace-of-mind package. The incident took months of wrangling to resolve, with the Caravelle eventually being repaired by a VW dealership over the border in Camporosso, Italy.

And on the Monday, after her first day at *maternelle*, our daughter threw herself into her mum's arms and said, crying:

'That wasn't fun at all.'

* * *

Maud adjusted, as children do. Within a week she had a few words of French, and some friends. The palaver over repairs to the Caravelle meant we had to have a hire car for two months, but there was an upside: we bought bikes.

This meant I would cycle Maud to and from *maternelle* each day, along the seafront, and not once did I take the joy of this routine for granted. But just as we were beginning to settle and head off on weekends to explore, along came France's second major Covid lockdown.

Beginning on 17 October 2020, the majority of public establishments were closed. An overnight curfew was imposed in most of France, from 9pm to 6am. Masks had been mandatory in public places since our arrival, but there was a variation from the ban on all essential travel in the first lockdown in France (which ran from 17 March 2020 to 10 May 2020): we were now only able to travel, for certain designated reasons, within a 20km radius of our residence. But unlike the first lockdown, primary and secondary schools remained open.

Lockdown in Menton was greeted with a prevailing impassivity. People congregated at bars and cafes as usual, only to hover next to tall tables placed outside rather than sit inside. Exercise was permitted, as were many other activities. We could go shopping. We could walk the dogs. Maud's *maternelle* remained open, and on the daily school run as many parents disdained to wear masks as those who played by the rules. The evening curfew made no dent on our lives: with a three-year-old in tow, we weren't exactly desperate for nightlife. I have a feeling it didn't much affect our friends either, all of whom we met through Maud's school. No one was champing at the bit for a major night out.

But the 20km restriction on travel meant our sorties into Italy and west along the French Riviera came to an end, and it was during this period that I began to swim, first, three times a week, then four to five, until finally I'd developed a routine of swimming a mile each day. I'd miss the odd day but swimming became an obsession. If I didn't swim, it felt as if something was missing. Soon enough, I realised that swimming was meditative. It was its absence of thought, combined with simple physicality, that so captivated me. I needed it as an antidote to the stress of work, the stress of my French not being up to scratch, the stress of my 'Serenity Abroad' insurance cover; the stress of things like people driving into your vehicle for no reason, underwriters trying to weasel their way out of meeting the repair bill, my serial failure to comprehend Vincent, Blondine and Christel, the trio in L'Amie du Pain, our local cafe and *boulangerie* (why, I would constantly ask myself as I walked away with our daily *paillasse* baguette, do they insist on speaking so fast? Do the locals understand them?).

I also needed swimming as the only exercise I could do after I wrecked my right knee on a cycle ride to St Agnès, Europe's highest coastal village. It was a foolish exploit. I'd read of the Menton to St Agnès climb being a regular training route for Tour de France cyclists, the quickest of whom did it in under half an hour. I wondered if I could manage it, the answer to which was yes, but in an hour and at the expense of the meniscus in my right knee. The scans suggested an operation would be necessary. First, though, I'd have to rest and see if it recovered. Either way, the end of football had finally arrived. There was no way I could play with a knee that hurt so much, and which I couldn't extend fully. But I could still swim. Neither lockdown nor my knee could stop me.

I kept swimming, through lockdown and its variants, into spring and summer 2021 and the lifting of Covid restrictions, and each day during the delayed UEFA Euro 2020. By then, I'd met John O'Hare, a 6ft 4in man who was as big and bearlike as QPR's Phil Parkes. We'd watch games together and talk about the days we'd had, the beauty of the French Riviera, our dreams for our children. And swimming. I always had the feeling that John wanted to swim as much as I did, but somehow things always got in the way. 'You and your swimming,' he said, more than once.

Swimming was the one time of the day when I didn't think about a single thing.

Except that day, in the middle of 2021's Euro 2020, when Stan Bowles swam into my mind. *Stan played on the Med.* What did he make of it? Was he charmed by Mediterranean life? Today, would a player of Bowles's calibre spend a couple of years playing for the likes of Monaco, Nice or, as had a few British players, Sampdoria? Did he and the other QPR players who took on AEK Athens in the Greek capital even see anything of the Med? Or did they just fly to Athens, play the game and fly back to London again?

I knew, even as I continued my swim, that my mind was playing a trick. I wanted Stan Bowles to have loved the Med. I wanted him to declare, 'Why, yes, of course, I'd have loved to play for Sampdoria or Monaco or Nice or, frankly, any club on the Med. What a place it is!'

This delusional merging of hero and self is doubtless fertile ground for psychoanalysis. The second thought, on that swim from France to Italy and back, was more straightforward. It was this:

Here I am, lucky enough to live in Menton on the French-Italian border, and a new football season starts in about a month. My knee has had it. Even if there is a five-a-side scene here, I won't be playing football again. But – thank God – lockdown is over. I could get to and from games along the French and Italian Rivieras in a day. Monaco is on my doorstep, Nice is half an hour away. Is Marseille on the Riviera? I don't know, but, wow, to go and watch Olympique de Marseille! It's a two-hour drive. And there's Genoa and Sampdoria in Italy. And Spezia – aren't they in Serie A? There must be loads of clubs in lower divisions. Does Cannes have a football team? Antibes? Menton itself? What about Ventimiglia, the first town in Italy when you've crossed the border? And Sanremo – it's a sizeable place, there must be a club there. On to Imperia, past Genoa to Sestri Levante. All these places, hosting football matches on the Med, along this beautiful coastline, a place I first visited as a 15-year-old and whose allure made me return to make it home, all these years later. How does the Med influence football? Is it a little more blessed, a little more beautiful? The fans, the players, the owners – are they calmer, more benign, than their counterparts from northern Europe?

I knew, as I finished that swim, how the 2021/22 football season would play out for me.

I'd have a season on the Med. If I could, I'd make a pilgrimage to Athens. I'd go to the Nikos Goumas Stadium. I'd watch AEK Athens. I'd do this to honour my hero, Stan Bowles.

1

August 2021

Out of the Soup

IT WOULD be a season on the Med, but it would begin in England. Covid meant we hadn't seen our families and friends for months, so we needed to return to the UK as soon as Maud's summer term finished. This ended up being a six-week trip, taking up the latter part of July and all of August 2021. I missed the game I'd had in mind to kick things off, fortuitously because that's exactly what happened when Nice hosted Marseille on 22 August. It was mayhem. Total chaos. An encounter that might have made me think life isn't so chilled on the Med after all.

Instead, I saw two games in England that warmed my heart.

* * *

On a less-than-Mediterranean day, with passing cloud and occasional showers, I'm in Exmouth, East Devon. I guess the temperature is touching 14°C. I was brought up in Exmouth and its nearby town to the east, Budleigh

Salterton, and have returned not just to see my parents but a friend from the past. Rob Cox, a local builder, runs Lympstone Amateur Boxing Club – which, despite its name, is located in the middle of Exmouth – but I'm not here for boxing. Rob and I will be heading to the lesser-known St James Park in the afternoon, home of Exeter City rather than Newcastle United. We'll be there for Exeter v Bradford City, the opening game of the League Two season. The Grecians v the Bantams.

But first, it's a drive along Exmouth seafront. It's a world away from the place I knew as a teenager. Then, there was a sense of faded Victorian grandeur teetering towards dilapidation. Now, trendy beachside bars and shops serve the hordes of kite-surfers who've transformed the town. Rob's house – light, airy, modern – is on a hill overlooking the action. Inside, Rob and I talk boxing. His is a family of serious boxing pedigree. His grandfather, Jack Cox, was a pro boxer from 1925 to 1934; at one point, he was the West of England heavyweight champion. Rob's father, Chris, was on the undercard of the first of the two great Henry Cooper v Muhammad Ali fights, at Wembley Stadium on Tuesday, 18 June 1963. In those days, Ali went by his given name, Cassius Clay.

Like father, like son: Exeter-based Chris was boxing as a heavyweight. It would prove to be his 12th and last professional fight, against Leicester boxer Mick Basten (spelt Bastin in the flyer for the event). The fight didn't happen on the night of Cooper's memorable fourth-round left hook to Ali's jaw, a pulverising punch that lifted him off his feet and sent him, via the ropes, to the canvas. But for the cushion of the ropes, would Ali have been out for the count? Possibly. Should Rob's father have called time on his career when, in a rescheduled bout at Wembley Empire two days after Clay won in the fifth round against Cooper, he lost on points?

Rob himself never turned pro, instead racking up multiple amateur bouts. Today, aged 53, he is genial, courteous, hospitable, but he oozes strength and power. Not even in my own, far more modest, boxing heyday would I have fancied sparring with him. But if it was boxing all the way for Rob, his father and his brothers, Rob's son has a different future.

Sonny Cox – tall, lithe, black-haired, athletic – sits on the sofa, watching sport on TV, as Rob, his wife Amanda and I talk. Sonny has been playing football since he could walk. He radiates calm. Confidence, too. No wonder: a year earlier, a couple of days before we set off for Menton, I'd seen him score a hatful of goals for Exeter City in an Under-15 match against Taunton Town. On Exeter City's books for the past few years, Sonny is a goalscoring machine. He can play with either foot. He's quick-thinking, skilful, fast. And lately, he's gone from strength to strength. Premier League clubs want to sign him. He has a trial coming up with Manchester United. Then there's another one with Brighton & Hove Albion; yet another with Chelsea.

Sonny is tipped not just as a future Premier League player, but an England player too. 'I like boxing, but prefer football,' says Sonny, picking up the tail-end of my conversation with his father. I tell him this is a sensible preference. 'Boxing hurts too much,' I say. Sonny laughs. He can't come with Rob and me to City today.

'Covid restrictions,' he says. How does he feel about the top clubs circling? Will City let him go, or hold on to a prize asset? Sonny smiles and shrugs. 'Let's see what happens,' he says.

On the drive from Exmouth to Exeter, I tell Rob I've rarely met a more laid-back 16-year-old. And I've definitely never met a teenager with the self-confidence to look ahead to Premier League trials as if he was nipping out for a gentle stroll along Exmouth seafront. 'Nothing fazes him,' says Rob. 'Nothing at all.' It's almost as if he's as proud of his son's sangfroid as his ability on a football pitch.

St James Park has a healthy attendance for City's clash against Bradford; 5,605 fans have turned up to the 8,696-capacity ground that has come and a long way from its ramshackle former self. Beginning at Sonny's age, I'd take the train from Exmouth with a friend called Rich and cheer on the Grecians on most Saturdays over a couple of seasons. It was a great day out, and an easy one too, given that St James Park train station is a stone's throw from the pitch. Tony Kellow was our hero back then. I ask Rob who to look out for today. 'The captain, Matt Jay,' he tells me. 'Decent player.'

And so, as I sit near the touchline in the IP Office Stand (a name that's not a patch on The Cowshed, its moniker as the terraced home of City diehards when I used to go to games), it proves from Jay's first touch. He's a clever player who's been with City since 2003. Aged 25 as we watch, Jay made his professional debut in 2013. He's an attacking midfielder with a healthy approximate ratio of a goal for every three games. At 5ft 6in, Jay is small, but he's ultra-fit, reads the game well and pulls City's strings. But if Jay is City's heart, the team's new keeper, Cameron Dawson, keeps them in it with an outstanding double save midway through the first half, denying first Callum Cooke and then Sheffield Wednesday loanee Lee Angol. Moments later, Dawson is again a match for Angol.

It's 0-0 at half-time. I take a look around St James Park. Like Exmouth seafront, it's been redeveloped. Opposite the IP Office Stand is the impressive Adam Stansfield Stand, opened in October 2018. Rob tells me the Cowshed went a long time ago: the IP Office Stand – all-seater, covered, running the length of the pitch, was opened in 2001. Even before then, the old Big Bank, behind the home fans' goal, had changed. Opened in February 2000, with a capacity of 3,950 and covered, it's the largest terrace left in the English Football League. I'd been to a couple of QPR away games at City since my teenage years, but hadn't clocked the changes. Pleasingly, the old away end on St James' Road seems as rickety as ever.

At one of those City v QPR games, a League Cup clash on 11 August 2009 won 5-0 by the Hoops, an ageing man shuffled the length of each touchline. I recognised him at once. It was Norman Shiel, who taught classics at Exeter School. For a reason I no longer recall, I opted for Ancient Greek A-level when at the school. I was useless at it, achieving what was probably a sympathetic E grade, but, as the only pupil in Norman's class, I won the school's Ancient Greek prize two years running. A Geordie, Norman had been a football nut; when I was at school, there were rumours he'd played for Blyth Spartans. He'd fallen in love with the Grecians upon moving to

Exeter in the late-1980s, and has contributed a lifetime's memorabilia to The Grecian Archive. If anyone would know the origin of English football's quirkiest nickname, surely it would be Norman.

I didn't speak to him as he wandered past the QPR fans, 12 years ago. Now, I look in vain. There's no sign of Norman. I never knew what he was doing walking the length of each touchline, but it would be good to see him today. In Norman's absence, I defer to checking the Exeter City website on my phone. This is tantalising rather than conclusive. I learn that City began life in 1901 as St Sidwell's United, given their origins in Exeter's St Sidwell's area. They adopted St James Park as their home ground in 1903, when they joined the East Devon Senior League. Then, on 31 May 1904, it was decided to change the name to Exeter City Association Football Club – with the proviso that the club nickname, the Grecians, would be kept.

As the club's website has it: 'People from the St Sidwell's area of Exeter traditionally referred to themselves as Greeks or Grecians as they live outside the old walls of the city.'

It took further scrolling to discover more. Apparently, according to a book called *Exeter Past* by Hazel Bond, a fair took place in Exeter's Southernhay district in 1726. At this fair, there was a re-enactment of the siege of Troy. Those who lived within the city's old Roman walls played the part of the Trojans, those beyond – in the St Sidwell area – were the Greeks.

Is this true? I look again for Norman. He is nowhere to be seen. The second half ebbs and flows. Both sides play passing football, looking to play the ball on the ground even from the depths of defence. Years ago, it would have been hoofed into the stands.

The game ends in a 0-0 draw, one that genuinely merits the adjective 'entertaining'. Dawson is the man of the match. Rob and I drive back to Exmouth, talking football, boxing and Sonny. What's best for this prodigiously talented 16-year-old? Even if City were to release him – which is a big if – might he disappear amid the scores of players on the books at clubs like Manchester United and Chelsea? If he stays at City, how far away is he from being a first-team regular? Could a non-league loan spell be a good idea?

Neither Rob nor I are sure. But it's a fair bet Sonny will shrug and say, 'Let's see what happens'.

* * *

It's the end of a hot August day in London. It's as warm as the Med. I've had a day of meetings, it's humid, I'm tired, and enthusiasm for tonight's QPR game has waned. We're at home to Oxford United in the EFL Cup. Not a must-see game. I ring Caroline, who's with our daughter at her father's place in Wiltshire. All is well. I mutter about not bothering with QPR tonight. I have more meetings the following morning and will be staying the night in London; maybe I should retreat to my hotel and get some rest. Caroline is insistent, 'You love QPR. What else are you going to do? Sit in your hotel room, staring at the walls? You'll love it when you're there.'

Caroline is right. I've racked up 40 years of going to Loftus Road (I wish I could get used to calling it the Kiyan Prince Foundation Stadium, but the Loftus Road habit is hard to break) and every time I go there, it feels like home. I've never had a season ticket, always been just a club member (and have let that lapse since we moved to France). So instead of what I imagine is a deep joy – sitting in the same spot, week in, week out – I'll end up anywhere: in either the Lower or Upper Loft, in the South Africa Road stand, in the Ellerslie Road stand, in the West or East Paddocks, even in the School End if I have to (the School End is the away end, though sometimes it has an area for home fans). Tonight, I plump for the Ellerslie Road, and as I push through the turnstile there's that familiar tingle in my spine. This is the place. I'm back. This is home.

Oxford United are in League One, and while I bear them no animosity, the club always prompts a couple of peculiar associations. The obvious one is QPR's loss to Oxford in the 1986 League Cup Final. I watched the game in the common room at the University of East Anglia, with my QPR scarf and girlfriend at the time, Stephanie. Oxford were the underdogs, and I was the lone QPR fan. We didn't turn up that day and lost 3-0. It was embarrassing.

Then there was an away game at Oxford's ground one Saturday in September 1998. I met a friend there, Richard – like me a lifelong Hoop. I'd brought along my elder son, Harry. He was just over three then. He had a Matchbox car, I can't remember what kind. As we were walking to the game he was driving it along walls, along shop windows, up and down shop doors. A benign enough activity, but I should have stopped him because he decided to post the car through the letterbox of a shop. The shop was shut. It wouldn't reopen until Monday. We did not live near Oxford, and wouldn't be coming back to the shop on Monday. Or any other day. Harry tried but couldn't process the eternal loss of the car. We plodded on to the game. By the time we reached the queue at the turnstiles, Harry was inconsolable. The QPR fans were sympathetic. 'Does he know something we don't?' said one.

Perhaps he did. The Rs went on to lose 4-1.

To this day, the fate of Harry's car pops into my mind. What happened to it? What did the shopkeeper think when he or she saw it there on the floor at the beginning of Monday's trade? I like to think a lucky – so lucky! – child was the beneficiary. I don't like to think of the car being tossed in a bin. What with the traumatic loss of his car and the team his dad supports shipping four goals, maybe it's no surprise that Harry didn't go on to be a football fan.

Tonight, though, the Rs are on form. As for the Grecians v the Bantams, I watch football that's radically different from that which dominated the English game when I was growing up. Both sides are well organised and keep their shape. Neither looks to play long balls. Even defenders under pressure want to play their way out of trouble. It's a treat, and even more so when, in the 26th minute, Rob Dickie hits a screamer for Rangers' first goal. Surging forward in the middle of the pitch, the former Oxford man unleashes a rocket, à la Ronnie Radford's famous strike for Hereford United against Newcastle United in the FA Cup third-round replay tie of 1972. Like the Radford rocket, not a keeper in the world could have kept out Dickie's bomb. The Rs ease 2-0 ahead in the

40th minute thanks to an Oxford own goal. They cruise through the second half to a healthy win.

I leave, happy, but not just because my side won or because they played crisp, passing football. The former is always welcome, the latter has, save for occasional lapses, been the club's way ever since the great Dave Sexton side of the early- to mid-1970s. No, it's the panache of each of Exeter City, Bradford City and Oxford United. English football has changed. Is it – whisper it quietly – a little continental nowadays?

* * *

The mud was outrageous. Dense and soupy, it sucked the ball into its dank, dark creases. Both sets of players were confounded, time and again. They'd expect the ball to bounce, but it wouldn't. They'd think it would skim off the surface, but it refused. Phil Parkes, the QPR goalkeeper, had it bad. A high ball loomed overhead, and he took a step or two backwards, watching it all the way. Rather than bounce and angle upwards into his giant hands, the ball thudded into the brown quicksand of Parkes's penalty area – and stayed there. With a shake of his head, the big man stooped to pick it up.

Nowadays, a professional game wouldn't happen in the mud-bath that was Ashton Gate, Bristol City's ground, on 19 March 1977. Not in the Premier League, anyway. Today's stars wouldn't risk their superannuated ankles in such appalling conditions. But this was the First Division in the 1970s, and things were different then. Very different. Truth is, too, that I didn't care about the mud. I didn't care about the cold and the wisps of rain in the air, either. I didn't care about the crush of the crowd on the terrace, and although I noted it – it was impossible not to – I didn't care about the language of the fans around me (more obscene than anything I've heard since, anywhere).

All I cared about, as a boy of ten, was seeing QPR and Stan Bowles, the club's resident genius, play in the flesh.

It was a birthday treat. In nine days, I'd turn 11, and Dad was taking me and two friends to see QPR play for the first time. The night before we set off for Bristol, I barely slept. I was awake at 3am, looking at my radio alarm clock, sighing that it wasn't time to get up. Awake again at 4am, I got up and went downstairs, as if I might hasten the dawn. No good, nothing for it but to go back to bed. Soon it was five o' clock, but as dark as ever outside. But then it was 7am, and with the faintest half-light slipping through the curtain I could justify getting up. I had a football-sized foam dice in my room, a legacy of Christmas. I would use it as a football, scoring goals with shots angled under an old desk, or, at the other, away end, if they swept in under the window ledge. I was usually Stan Bowles, sometimes Gerry Francis or Dave Thomas, two other QPR stars. Strangely, there was an imaginary opponent called Gonzalez. Where he came from I don't know. That morning, bedroom football was more urgent than ever. I was Stan Bowles, tricking Bristol City's defenders (sans Gonzalez – he didn't feel right for this game), shimmying back and forth, nutmegging them for fun, scoring with impossible back-heels and netting a hat-trick so perfect that the only words needed were, in ITV *Big Match* commentator Brian Moore's voice, 'Stanley Bowles.'

The way Moore said it, it was as if those words were complete in themselves. Nothing else was necessary. Any other language was as futile as the efforts of so many of the defenders of the 1970s, when they were pitted against Stan. It was just Stanley Bowles, the words, the man, the skill, the flair: the statement of genius as constant as it was casual.

My friends, Elliot and Peter, knew nothing of this. Football, whether in a bedroom with a foam dice, at school, in parks or on TV, wasn't their thing. But I'd convinced everyone – well, my dad, my friends, and my friends' parents – that QPR playing away at Bristol City was as good as it gets. This would be the best birthday treat, ever.

Exmouth was a long way from Loftus Road, QPR's ground in west London, but a fairly short hop up the M5 to Bristol. That was the good news for me as a QPR fanatic and for my dad as the person in charge of getting me and my friends to the game. The bad news? Dad had never been to a football match in his life. Now here he was, about to ferry three pre-pubescent boys up the motorway. He felt apprehensive.

'I wasn't sure what to expect,' he told me, years later. 'The papers were full of stories of violence and hooligans. But you wanted to go to that game at Bristol as your birthday present. You'd become obsessed with football. And with QPR.'

Obsessed I was, despite my parents being blind to the game's charms. They're weren't sporty types, though if anything Dad was a rugby man. But around nine, going on ten, playtime for me was about one thing, and one thing only: kicking a football. I watched *Football Focus* avidly, bought and read every issue of *Shoot!*, never missed *Final Score* and, on Saturday nights, I would beg and cajole my parents into letting me watch *Match of the Day* (usually unsuccessfully). I loved Sundays, Brian Moore and *The Big Match*. And like kids all over the world, I gravitated towards success. Liverpool! How could I follow any other team? They won everything. There's little so alluring as reflected glory when you're a child under ten.

Later in life, Mum and Dad completed a genealogical trawl of their ancestors and discovered that Dad's family had helped found Everton.

To think: if Dad had known that, if the football gene deep in his background hadn't skipped a couple of generations, I would have had an eye not on Liverpool's fortunes but on those of their sworn rivals from Goodison Park. But as it was, Grandad Harry set me on the path to Loftus Road.

I loved Harry. He was small, wiry man with endless patience and kindness. Better yet, he loved football. He was a Carlisle United fan and a tidy winger in his day. Family mythology had elevated Harry's skills to professional level. Later I learned this was untrue – that Grandad Harry might have *come from* Carlisle, but he hadn't *played football for* Carlisle. No matter. One wintry afternoon Harry walked into the sitting room to watch *Final Score* and was surprised to find me already there, glued to the teleprinter. He was even more surprised when I told him I was a Liverpool fan.

'You can't support Liverpool, Alec,' he said. 'You have to support the club you were born closest to.'

I liked this idea, and I liked that it came from Harry. A Maths teacher by profession, he soon saw an opportunity for me to learn something arithmetical. I was told to go and fetch a ruler and the London A-Z. And then, having found my place of birth – Chiswick Maternity Hospital – Harry made me measure the distance from it to Brentford, QPR, Fulham and Chelsea. I was born closest to Loftus Road, the home of Queens Park Rangers.

The day I discovered this was Saturday, 15 November 1975. QPR drew 1-1 away to Ipswich. Don Givens, capped 56 times by the Republic of Ireland, scored. It was to be one of many Givens goals in an illustrious QPR career, and it was scored in the club's greatest-ever season – 1975/76.

We so nearly won the league that year. We played continental, passing football. We had a poetry-loving manager who was way ahead of his time. We sparkled, we shone, we dazzled. And in a team of first-rate footballers, there was one who wore the number ten shirt.

Ten. The shirt of creativity. Of possibility. Of bewitching talent and bewildering skill. Of dreams made, and dreams shattered.

Stanley Bowles.

* * *

Many years later, a friend gave me Bowles's phone number. By this time, having begun my professional life as a lawyer, I was a freelance journalist. I'd scored a piece for a lads' mag on Bowles, a jokey interview on his life, times, winners, losers and all-round mishaps. I was thrilled. All these years later, and I'd finally speak to my childhood hero.

A quiet, indiferent voice answered the phone. I explained who I was and what I wanted, adding, 'It's such an honour to talk to you. You were my hero as a kid. I spent hours trying to do what you could do with a ball. I just wanted to be you.'

Stan didn't say anything. I blurted out a bit more undiluted praise, 'I just thought everything you did was amazing, and that you were the best footballer in England.'

'That's nice,' said Stan.

He said yeah, sure, he'd be up for an interview. But then added:

'What about the dough?'

This threw me. There'd been no word from my editor about paying Bowles for his time. And given the slim pickings I was being offered, I knew there'd be nothing on the table. It'd be pointless to ask.

Stan said he wanted £350.

I said I'd see what I could do.

My editor said, 'Nothing doing.'

I never got to interview Stan, and we never spoke again.

It didn't matter. I realised, a few years later, that Stan had done enough for me when I was a boy. His job was complete by the time I reached my teens. Stan, and Queens Park Rangers, had by then already taken me away from a path that was otherwise neatly laid out. It was a path that was never intended to involve football, but my life has been bound up with it ever since. I've seen great games, I've seen awful ones; I've played a lot and I've met people on the pitch who've become lifelong friends; I've suffered, I've been in ecstasy. And, like every fan, I think there's something special about *my club*.

Perhaps there is, maybe it's all an illusion. But I know one thing for sure. QPR, and football, is a broader church than people imagine.

In fact, the game is the broadest church of all.

I have Grandad Harry to thank for QPR, Stan Bowles and the joy, beauty and despair that has flowed ever since. My grandad, who got out the A-Z and a ruler, and made me do a simple bit of maths. My grandad, who I fancy would have loved a season on the Med. And who would have deplored what happened in the game I missed because of our trip to England.

The trouble began shortly after the 7.45pm kick-off on Sunday, 22 August 2021. Nice v Marseille pits two of France's biggest clubs against each other, and there's local pride at stake given they're separated by some 125 miles. More than that: if Marseille is traditionally associated with left-wing politics, not so much Nice. A spicy encounter is always to be expected, but the optimists among us felt this one might pass off peaceably. After all, this was the first game in 18 months at Nice's Allianz Riviera stadium which would be attended by fans. Some 32,000 arrived, and you'd be forgiven for thinking there'd be a fanfare of post-lockdown *joie de vivre*.

Not so. Bottles were thrown at Marseille players by fans in Nice's Populaire Sud end – the home of the club's most hardcore ultras – from early in the match. The stadium announcer asked them to stop, to no avail. Eventually, in the 75th minute, and with Nice leading 1-0 thanks to a superb goal by Danish international Kasper Dolberg, one hit Dmitri Payet, the former West Ham United striker who returned to Marseille from the Hammers in 2017.

Payet hurled it with as much force as he could muster back into the crowd. Not content with this, he did the same with another bottle. You can expect a number ten to be a bit different, but despite the provocation Payet broke a golden rule: never meet fan violence in kind. Predictably, Nice's ultras did not fall into stunned silence, one of regret, shame and self-mortification. They invaded the pitch and confronted the Marseille team, two of whom, Arsenal loanee Matteo Guendouzi and defender Álvaro González, had been quick to join Payet in making their own feelings known. For good measure, González blasted the ball with his left foot at the incensed Nice supporters.

The ensuing chaos made for astonishing scenes. Fans fought players. Players fought players. Marseille manager Jorge Sampaoli had to be restrained and led away, not just by his coaching staff but also, ironically, by Payet. Photographs later emerged of injuries to Marseille players, most notably scratch marks on Payet's back and a bloody cut to Luan Peres's neck. Amid the mayhem, Nice's captain, Brazilian veteran Dante, tried to reason with the ultras, ushering them back to the stands. Nice's president, Jean-Pierre Rivère, appealed for calm. Another outbreak of aggression occurred between the players as they left the pitch. It continued outside the dressing rooms. Then, Sampaoli was spotted wearing a backpack, clearly intent on leaving the scene. Bizarrely, the game restarted, a full 90 minutes after the pitch invasion, with only Nice's players on the pitch. Cue the referee's easiest decision of a tumultuous night: to abandon the match.

The aftermath was dominated by the blame game. Pablo Longoria, president of Marseille, criticised Ligue 1.

'We need to set precedents for French football,' he said. 'The referee was with us. He confirmed to us that safety was not assured. His decision was to abandon the match, but the LFP decided to restart the match. That is not acceptable for us.' Rivère had a different view. For him, 'the reaction of two Marseille players' had 'instigated things'. He added, 'It's disappointing that it ends like this. Things are quite clear. Marseille's security should not have come on to the pitch and hit our players. I don't really understand why Marseille didn't restart.'

The upshot, within two weeks, was a two-point penalty for Nice (one of which was suspended). Nice would also have to play three games behind closed doors. González was suspended for two games. Pablo Fernandez, Marseille's physio and a particularly enthusiastic member of their aggrieved coaching staff, was suspended for the rest of the season. Despite his prominent role, France's governing body for football, the Ligue de Football (LFP) felt a one-match suspended ban for Payet was enough.

As the governing body put it: 'Meeting this Wednesday, the Disciplinary Commission of the LFP ruled on the incidents which punctuated the match of the third day of Ligue 1 Uber Eats between OGC Nice and Olympique de Marseille.

'After reading the investigation report in the presence of the two clubs, the Commission decided to replay the match on a relocated field. In addition, two penalty points were imposed on OGC Nice, including one suspended point.

'Regarding the players, defender Álvaro González received two games of suspension. As for his team-mate Dimitri Payet, he was sanctioned with a suspended match.'

Nice v Marseille was replayed on Wednesday, 27 October 2021 at a neutral ground. It ended 1-1. By then, my season on the Med was well under way. I'd come to realise that Uber Eats, doubtless contractually entitled to its positioning in the LFP's statement, had a rival when it came to OGC Nice. '*Burger King: Le Restaurant Préféré Des Aiglons!*' screamed an ad in a Nice programme, '*Les Aiglons*' (The Eaglets) being Nice's nickname. I struggled with this, conceptually, because yes, Nice's fans might like a Whopper or two but the club's players? Surely not. But there was nothing to puzzle over in the first game I saw, on land reclaimed from the Mediterranean Sea. It was a belter.

2

September 2021

Aux Armes

THE STADE Louis II was rocking. It wasn't just the sound, it was the sheer physicality of the place. Thousands of people were jumping up and down, ceaselessly. Drummers at either end were thumping away. Outsized flags were being waved frenziedly as music blared and still, incredibly, hordes of bare-chested fans pogoed up and down. For the first time in my life, it struck me that you needed to be fit to be a football fan.

Or, to be precise, to be a fan of Olympique de Marseille. For here, in manicured Monaco, *Les Marseillais* had taken over. Their force was irresistible. Gamely, a hardcore of Monaco fans did their best to keep up but the truth was this: if you knew nothing of French football and had been plunged into the stadium, with no idea of who was at home and who was away, but had been told this game featured Marseille and Monaco, you'd have said, without a moment's hesitation, that Marseille were at home.

This game, on Saturday, 11 September, was the 100th league clash between two of Ligue 1's biggest clubs: the pair have 17 league titles between them, Marseille edging it with nine. Jorge Sampaoli's side had the better record going into the fixture, too. Despite the mayhem against Nice, the club variously known as OM, *Les Phocéens* and *Les Olympiens* had begun the season with an impressive 3-2 win away to Montpellier, following it with a 2-2 draw at home to Bordeaux and then a 3-1 win at home to Saint-Étienne. In contrast, AS Monaco, led by former Croatian team captain Niko Kovač, had a mere four points from their first four games. Neither side realistically expected to challenge super-spenders Paris Saint-Germain for the Ligue 1 title, but both had ambitions for a top-three finish, meaning guaranteed Champions League football for the second-placed side and entry to the third qualifying round for the team in third place.

History was on OM's side: Monaco have lost more home Ligue 1 games against Marseille than any other opponent (19 defeats in 51 games). Looking around the Stade Louis II, the reason for this was obvious. Marseille's fans were incredible. Their appearance swelled the home side's lacklustre average attendance of just under 6,000 to 8,615; the racket they kept up, alongside their constant movement, was phenomenal. Chants rang out all around Monaco's ground even before the game had begun, the first, and most rousing, being *Aux Armes*. The dominance of *Les Marseillais* was such that this was sung as a chorus and response, the first line from the designated away end, the echo from just about everywhere else in the stadium.

'*Aux Armes! Aux Armes! Nous sommes Les Marseillais et nous allons gagner. Allez l'OM!*'

Or, 'To arms! To arms! We are the people of Marseille and we're going to win.

Go, OM!'

It was impossible not to be swept away by the passion, the fervour, the sheer unquenchable belief. And cometh the hour, there was only one team in it: OM. From start to finish, Monaco were completely outclassed, so much so that by the end of the first half they had failed to have a single shot. The statistics would later reveal that Monaco had 51 per cent possession, from which they mustered seven shots (though not one was on target). But statistics be damned. OM's 49 per cent possession was a statistical sheep in wolf's clothing. They turned up and devoured Monaco.

For Dominique 'Doumé' Trefoloni, this wasn't how it was supposed to go. 'Monaco will win 1-0,' was Doumé's prediction, 20 minutes into the game. This was bold. OM had taken control from the first minute, with stand-in striker Bamba Dieng (in for the injured Polish player Arkadiusz 'Arek' Milik) hitting the post after a surging run in the 13th minute. The 21-year-old from Senegal, a Marseille player since October 2020, again hit the woodwork in the 29th minute, before scoring shortly before half-time after a pinpoint long ball from Brazilian defender Luan Peres. Dieng's pace and will were too much for the Monaco back line; his finish, a pacey right-footed drive, a textbook example of giving the keeper the eyes. Flat-footed, thinking the ball would go to his left, Monaco's German goalkeeper, Alexander Nübel, could only stick out a half-hearted knee as Dieng sent the ball low to his right.

Doumé continued to believe. I understood his hope, his indefatigable optimism. It's not as if being a lifelong QPR fan has made for a bursting trophy cabinet. Blind faith is often all there is. And so it was for Doumé as Marseille continued to batter Monaco. I felt for him. I'd met Doumé on the school run in Menton. He and his wife Cécile had shown us great kindness, whether it was running after us on perhaps our second weekend of living in Menton, insisting we shared a rum and coke on Les Sablettes (possibly the most child-friendly beach in France), inviting us to gigs in Peille, home of Doumé's jazz band, or for meals at Doumé's parents' retreat hidden amid the trees behind La Turbie, the hillside village high above Monaco. And if a parental 'retreat', coupled with Monaco, conjures a notion of the seemingly unlimited wealth for which the principality is renowned, Doumé and his family were true Monégasques, whose lives were a world away from those of the Formula 1 drivers, international businessmen and others among the super rich who'd decided to call Monaco home.

Doumé and Céci were both born in Monaco in 1980, while Doumé's father, Angelo (known to all as Ange), arrived in the 1930s: a communist, he left Italy to escape Mussolini and fascism, to work not as a yacht broker, or in Monaco's casino or its famed hotels and bars, or in its upmarket shops, or to idle away the days as a tax exile without need of work, but as a farmer on the heights of Beausoleil in an area named Grima, better known for Léo Ferré, an anarchist poet and singer, but also the place where Ange's parents already had a farm. Ange would sell the farm produce in Monaco's market at the foot of Le Rocher, in Condamine. 'My father told me that when he was young he used to ride a donkey to come home from the market,' Doumé once told me. 'My mother, Evelyne, met my father at this market one Labour Day, 1 May, when he was selling lilies.' Doumé's parents lived in an apartment in Monaco but kept a long, single-storey cabin in the La Turbie countryside, where they would spend weekends with their grandchildren, Clémence and Madeleine. They grew their own vegetables and each year Ange made orange wine, pipe in his mouth, with bitter oranges. Neither a swimming pool nor a TV were to be seen. Theirs was a rustic idyll that the residents for which Monaco is known would struggle to understand.

'I am Monaco until I am dead,' said Doumé, proudly wearing his red and white Monaco top. I fancied his devotion would be tested in the second half, so too my language skills. Doumé's French is impossibly thick, at once nasal and guttural; try to speak in his language as I often did, we would soon resort to English. I just couldn't make out the individual words in what came back at me. Doumé had a fair but less than perfect command of English. So it was that the prospect of 'Monaco 'til I die' became 'Monaco until I am dead', which doesn't have quite the rhythm of the English equivalent, fans in full voice opining they're 'Rangers [or whoever] 'til I die'.

But as much as Marseille pressed, as much as they were expected to miss Milik and the suspended Payet and yet thrived as if Dieng was the only striker they'd ever needed, as much as their fans kept pogoing and singing and jumping and chanting, still Doumé clung to hope. Even in the face of Dieng's second goal on the hour – again a textbook finish, this time a perfect example of using your body to hold off a defender, turn and shoot – Doumé was not beaten. His team were. *Les Rouges et Blancs* were out for the count. Nothing would see them embody the club mantra, on signs and hoardings – in English – around the Stade Louis II, 'Rise – Risk – Repeat'. The best they could hope for was damage limitation.

Even this seemed a stretch. If anything, Marseille's fans were now making even more noise. Certainly, they were still jumping, keen not to offend another frequent chant: '*Qui ne saute pas n'est pas Marseillais!*' Who doesn't jump is not from Marseille!

But in Doumé's eyes, there was still a flicker because, in the 67th minute, Dieng was substituted. Without this thorn in their side, could Monaco do it? Could they sneak a goal and snatch a draw? Would this ticket be €50 well spent, against all the odds? Alas for Doumé, no. OM closed out the game in the final 20 minutes, not so much parking the bus as moving it at will around the pitch, effortlessly neutralising such scant threat as Monaco could manage. Afterwards Dieng was elated, and yet humility itself, declaring, 'I'm happy with the performance and I thank the whole team and also the coach for trusting me.'

Doumé was phlegmatic. 'Next time, we have better luck,' he said, as we walked along the harbour front near the Stade Louis II. Here were the fabled yachts of Monaco's millionaires. Next to them, a flotilla of Ferraris and Lamborghinis. Even when Bernie Ecclestone and Flavio Briatore loomed large at QPR, I'd never seen a car worth half a million sterling parked outside Loftus Road. I counted at least five as we made our way along the Fontvielle harbour to the Ship & Castle, where Doumé suggested a post-match beer. Earlier we'd visited Slammers bar on Rue Suffren-Reymond in the centre of Monaco. It was full of expats with designer clothes, expensive watches and bulging midriffs. The music was loud, the conversation ephemeral, the barman nice but the space too small. The thought of being stuck in Slammers during the Monaco Grand Prix was terrifying.

The Ship & Castle – very much modelled on the traditional English pub – made for a pleasant change. Again, however, I felt sorry for Doumé, though this time not because his team had lost. He was as entitled to call Monaco home as anyone. But was this tiny sovereign state, one of the wealthiest places in the world, really home? Did Doumé look up to Albert II, Prince of Monaco, second son of Prince Rainer III and Grace Kelly and competitor in five Winter Olympics for Monaco (bobsleigh), with nothing but admiration? Was Prince Albert's estimated $1bn in assets a source of pride? I knew enough of Doumé by now to know that he loved jazz, played good jazz bass, was a teacher and liked Jack Kerouac. And that he loved AS Monaco as much as any fan loves their club.

As we climbed into his red Nissan Micra to head the few miles back to Menton, I asked Doumé what he made of Monaco and its glitz, money and myth.

'I wouldn't want to live here,' he said. 'I prefer Menton.'

3

September 2021

Beautiful Confusion

JOHN AND I couldn't believe our eyes. The Navigator was amazed, too. What we were witnessing was really happening, and it really wouldn't happen at an English league game. Sure, players take off their shirts and throw them into the crowd. But their shorts?

We'd tracked a cameraman and camerawoman walking across the pitch at the end of Genoa's home match against Fiorentina. The woman was carrying the large, black camera on her shoulder, the man its trailing cable. All but a scattering of the players had long since left the pitch. The last man to go was Giacomo 'Jack' Bonaventura, scorer of the game's winning goal. The 32-year-old midfielder had earned his nickname not just because Jack is an Anglicised diminutive of Giacomo, but also by way of a nod to the game of poker. When a jack hits the table, a player is often set fair, although not if it's accompanied by a four. Jack-Four is known as 'Full Employment', because if you play it in Texas Hold 'Em you'll always have a day job. None of us realised that Jack, very happy with his day job on 18 September 2021, was the object of the camera pair's attention.

Beneath us on the halfway line in the wonderful Stadio Luigi Ferraris – surely one of Europe's greatest stadia – Bonaventura stopped, listened and smiled at the words said by the camera folk. And then, without a moment's hesitation, he slid out of his white, slightly muddied shorts and gave them to the camerawoman. I can't recall if they then embraced. I know the smiles continued. All the way across to the other side of the pitch, the woman kept laughing and joking with her colleague as she clutched her prized new possession.

* * *

My love affair with the Mediterranean began in Genoa.

I was 15. Mum and Dad – perhaps ambitiously, now I look back on it – had taken my brother, sister and me on a road trip through western Europe for our summer holiday. Not for them the easy option of a package holiday to Majorca (although we did that one year and met Brian Clough, who lost no time in telling Mum he'd like to spend more time with her – not, I realise now, because he wanted to debate the finer points of football formations). No. We would drive through France, Luxembourg, Germany, Liechtenstein, Italy and then back home through the middle of France.

I can remember little of the trip. I recall a bad crash on the way home on the Route du Soleil and, somewhere along the banks of the River Rhine, Dad stopping next to a vineyard and sampling some grapes. That's about it, save for two places: Menton and Genoa.

We arrived in the Italian port late one afternoon with nowhere to stay. We stopped and asked receptionists in hotel after hotel. Nothing doing. Tempers were fraying, but I was captivated. What a place this was! A huge harbour, monumental ships, narrow alleyways disappearing into a dense and seemingly impenetrable old town, restaurants, colour, sound, people of all kinds everywhere. It was unlike anything I'd known in Britain. I stared out of the car window, mesmerised, as we kept driving west, out of the city, again and again finding nothing until finally, in the seaside town of Varazze some ten or 12 miles away, we got lucky. A small hotel had a couple of rooms. We checked in and stayed for four days.

On the first night, we ate in the hotel's restaurant. We were seated next to an Italian family. Mum and Dad struck up a conversation. An awkward, gauche teenager, I was too shy to contribute, but even more so than usual thanks to the Italian family's daughter. Of above average height and slender with long, blonde hair, she was beautiful. I blushed when our respective parents introduced us. The next day, I saw Cristina swim out to a floating raft, the kind that appear off Mediterranean beaches each summer. I was a good swimmer and wasn't worried about the distance, but needed some moral support, so persuaded Mum to swim out with me. Mum is a sociable soul and duly chatted away to everyone on the raft, including Cristina. Soon, despite my chronic shyness, I was also chatting away to Cristina (who spoke excellent English, to my non-existent Italian). With no offence to my mother intended, I was very keen for her to swim back to shore and leave us alone.

Cristina and I had a tender, inchoate romance for our remaining few days in Varazze. I was sad to leave, desolate even, in the way of teenagers when a holiday comes to an end but all the more so when romance is involved. We promised we'd send letters and keep in touch.

Our next stop was Menton, about an hour and a half heading west along the Italian Riviera and just over the border in France. I thought of nothing but Cristina all the way there. My memory of Menton is of a soothing blur of the ever-present blue of the sea.

* * *

Genoa, Cristina, the Med.

I always knew I'd come back, but I had no idea my return to Genoa would be to watch the oldest football club in Italy take on Fiorentina. But, some 40 years later, that was what I was doing on Saturday, 18 September 2021. With me were John O'Hare, a friend from Menton, and a young man called Alex Thompson, whom we'd met on the train from Menton via Ventimiglia to Genoa Piazza Principe, the city's main station. Easy-going and confident, Alex had recently decamped from the UK to Sanremo in Italy, where he'd taken a job working on a yacht as a deckhand. Saturday was his day off. A football fanatic, the obvious thing for Alex to do was take himself to Genoa to see a game. He would have preferred the local derby – Genoa v Sampdoria – but Tuscany's *La Viola* weren't a bad substitute.

Alex had a degree in Geography, so John and I put him in charge of getting us from the train station to the

Stadio Luigi Ferraris. Located in the Marassi area of Genoa, the stadium opened in 1911 and hosts not only Genoa but also their arch-rivals, Sampdoria. It took us 35 minutes to walk there from Genoa Piazza Principe, up and down many steep hills. But we took not one wrong turn, so Alex metamorphosed into The Navigator or, often enough, just Nav.

En route to the stadium, we kept seeing images of griffins, whether stickers on lamp-posts, posters or graffiti. Half -lion, half-eagle, the griffin features on the city of Genoa's coat of arms. There are two griffins, either side of the St George's Cross. Genoa Cricket and Football Club – to give it its full name – settled for a single, yellow griffin, against a backdrop of blue and red (the club colours) and beneath a St George's Cross.

Il Grifone, or the Griffins, as Genoa are known, have an illustrious history and their links to England lie far deeper than sharing the St George's Cross. Genoa's football club only came into being thanks to a group of Englishmen abroad. Their most prominent member was diplomat and writer Sir Charles Alfred Payton, who, in February 1893, became Britain's consul in Genoa. An adventurous man who once prospected for gold in California, Payton banded together with other English residents in the city to form Genoa Cricket and Athletic Club on 7 September 1893. The club's shirts were the same colour as those of the England national team – white – and it was established with the aim of representing British sporting interests abroad. A few years later, a Londoner would tweak the club's identity. James Richardson Spensley, a doctor who was working in Genoa to treat sailors from coal ships, created a new footballing section on 10 April 1897, becoming its first manager and also taking to the field occasionally himself. Across a decade at the helm, Spensley made 22 appearances, initially as a defender before opting to keep goal.

Genoa, Italy's first football club, won the national title in 1898, its first year, despite an inauspicious start. The club's first game, a friendly against a mixed team of players from Internazionale Torino and FBC Torinese played before a crowd of 154, ended in a 1-0 defeat. But under player-manager Spensley, the team would become all-conquering, dropping 'Athletic' from its name in 1899 and going on to be champions – in a competition organised via regional mini-leagues, with the winners going on to knockout stages (like the modern-day Champions League) in 1899, 1900, 1902, 1903 and 1905. Three more titles would follow, in 1915, 1923 and 1924, making for a total haul of nine.

To this day, Spensley – who was also a boxer and scout leader, co-founding the Italian scouting movement called Federazione Italiano dello Scautismo in 1910 – is feted by the Genovese. Near the Ristorante Pizzeria New O'Sole Mio, where we ate some pasta before the game, there is a road named after him (the Via James Richardson Spensley).

A plaque on Spensley's Genoa house reads: 'Here lived the English doctor James R. Spensley, sportsman – great friend of Italy – a football pioneer with the Genoa Cricket and Football Club, founder of Genoese scouting.'

Spensley died in the First World War in 1915, while serving in Germany as a lieutenant in the Royal Army

Medical Corps. He was injured while treating the wounds of an enemy soldier and died later in hospital at Mainz.

* * *

Under Spensley, Genoa became the first Italian football team to play an international match, travelling to France and beating Nice 3-0 on 27 April 1903. A convincing victory, but Fiorentina were likely to pose a sterner test, coming into the fixture on the back of two Serie A wins. In marked contrast, Genoa had shipped eight goals in three games, losing 4-0 away to Inter Milan on the opening day of the season, then losing 2-1 at home to Naples before nabbing a 3-2 win away to Cagliari. Would their defence be as leaky in this, their fourth Serie A outing?

As ever, the stats melted away as we entered the Stadio Luigi Ferraris. What a stadium! Four rectangular towers reach upwards in each corner, with white steel trusses supporting the roof (also white, though invisible from the streets below). A theme of square boxes is played out everywhere, whether compacted along the exterior, terracotta pitchside walls or as four larger square gaps in the external walls behind each goal. Within the ground, there are again boxes in the towers. The feeling of rigorous, geometric functionalism continues with square-shaped stairwells, and yet, despite vertiginous upper tiers, the Stadio Luigi Ferraris is, for me, Loftus Road on steroids. It dominates the chaotic streets of the Marassi, imposing order where there seems to be none. And wherever you are, the action feels so close it's as if you could reach out and touch the players.

The referee, Livio Marinello, had been predicted to let the game flow. By its end, he'd dished out a total of six yellow cards, the first of which went to Abdoulaye Touré, a French midfielder who'd signed for Genoa from Nantes a month earlier. The tackles were rugged throughout, but it's also fair to say that both sets of players knew how to make the most of them. Time and again a man would go down as if struck by a thunderbolt, to writhe in agony on the grass. Then, as if blessed by a miracle, he would be up and playing on. Marinello had his work cut out. A peculiar consequence was that the many stoppages made for some unexpected observations from John and Nav.

'Did you know that Genoa fans wear St George Cross shirts because their sailors used to wear them?' asked Nav, early in the first half. I did, but there was more. 'We, the English, stole the St George's Cross from them!'

English cultural appropriation is not unprecedented; if true, Nav's contention is perhaps not that startling. John, meanwhile, was focusing on the Italian language. 'Did you know that "ciao" means both hello and goodbye?' he asked. Yes, I did. Was this emblematic of a fundamental ambiguity, or ambivalence, in Italian culture? I had no idea. 'Well, think about it,' said John. 'Genoa share this ground with Sampdoria.'

John, a Liverpudlian, was also delighted, though silently so, when the home fans broke out into a rendition of 'Que Sera, Sera'. I looked at his face, beaming with this unexpected reminder of Anfield. 'I'm surprised you didn't say anything,' I said. 'I thought about it,' said John. 'But then I thought, "Whatever will be, will be".'

Rough and primitive, with Genoa's only threat to Fiorentina's slicker football seeming to come from set pieces, the game was goalless at half-time. High on a hill above us, visible from the three-tier Distinti stand, was a tall church. The weather was far from Mediterranean. Black clouds were deluging the city with torrents of rain. A man to my right had been chain-smoking throughout the first half. It didn't seem possible but now he seemed to smoke even more. I hunched closer to John to try and evade the omnipresent nicotine and chanced upon a note I'd made: the Stadio Luigi Ferraris, rebuilt for the 1990 World Cup, had inspired the redevelopment, from 1995 to 2008, of Preston North End's Deepdale Stadium.

Fiorentina's manager, Vincenzo Italiano, made a telling substitution. On came Riccardo Saponara, a muscular attacking midfielder. On the hour, with an assist by Bonaventura, Saponara cut inside from the left wing, beat two players and then smashed the ball into the top corner. Screams of 'bastardo!' rang out from the Genoa fans around us. I wasn't sure if their ire was aimed at Saponara or Touré, who, as Nav put it, was having a shocker and went missing during Fiorentina's build-up to the goal. Davide Ballardini, the Genoa manager, took him off in the 64th minute.

A little earlier, Ballardini had brought on the formidable, though ageing, Goran Pandev. The Macedonian striker, who'd spent most of his professional career in Italy, was easily Genoa's best player. Despite his 38 years, he contrived to find time and space, to beat a player and to make intelligent decisions. But pace was not his forte, and with the rest of his team looking even more pedestrian Pandev could not prevent what looked more and more like a certain Fiorentina win. The game was settled in the 89th minute, when Saponara returned the favour and assisted Bonaventura, cleverly flicking a pass on to him with the outside of his right boot. Bonaventura drilled the ball into the bottom right corner.

A dubious penalty in the eighth minute of added time was converted by Genoa's left-back, Domenico Criscito, to give *Il Grifoni* a consolation goal. Perhaps Marinello, in only his 12th Serie A game, felt sorry for the home side. Certainly, if Pandev had cleverly played in Milan Badelj, the Croatian midfielder seemed to take a couple of seconds before deciding to turn meagre contact from a defender into a dramatic, pain-laden pirouette. Was it a penalty? 'Softest I've ever seen,' said Nav. Italiano, a midfielder who'd played 196 times for Hellas Verona (and who'd briefly been a Griffin, making nine appearances for Genoa in 2005), wouldn't have cared. Fiorentina were worthy winners.

On the train back to Sanremo, for Nav, and Menton, for John and me, I wondered if Micah Richards would have been pleased, too: the right-back left Manchester City after they'd won the Premier League title in 2012 to join *La Viola*, the name given to the Florentine team because of their home colours, a rich purple ('viola' is Italian for purple). Beset by injuries, he made only ten appearances before returning to England to finish his career at Aston Villa. Did Richards, now a much-respected pundit in the UK, harbour a soft spot for Fiorentina? Perhaps one of his games had even been in Genoa, a city which seemed to me to be a tumultuous and exhausting accident, wholly lacking in anything resembling order and planning save for its scattering of palaces and churches and, in the heart of the Marassi, the extraordinary Stadio Luigi Ferraris.

Elsewhere, everywhere, was chaos, and physically draining chaos at that: if Rome was built on seven hills, there must be about 100 in Genoa.

Still, though, I loved the city. Mine was not a Dickensian conversion. I'd loved Genoa when I sat in the back of Mum and Dad's car, driving through the city aged 15. I loved it again now, visiting 40 years later. Dickens detested Genoa at first sight. Visiting in 1844, he wrote in *Pictures of Italy* that the centre was 'a maze of the vilest squalor, steaming with unwholesome stenches, and swarming with half-naked children and whole worlds of dirty people'. Genoa's houses were 'immensely high, painted in all sorts of colours, and are in every stage and state of damage, dirt, and lack of repair'. He wasn't keen on the proprietor of Villa Bagnarello, where he stayed initially in Genoa, referring to him as a drunken butcher and his villa as a 'pink jail'. But after ten weeks, Dickens escaped and moved into Villa Pallavicino, an altogether grander affair, with Renaissance frescoes and sumptuous grounds, commanding a view of much of what Dickens, even in his earlier billeting in Villa Bagnarello, had called the 'noble bay of Genoa, with the deep blue Mediterranean'. Now Dickens began to appreciate Genoa's charms – perhaps unsurprisingly, given where he ended up living for much of 1844:

'It stands on a height within the walls of Genoa, but aloof from the town: surrounded by beautiful gardens of its own, adorned with statues, vases, fountains, marble basins, terraces, walks of orange-trees and lemon-trees, groves of roses and camellias. All its apartments are beautiful in their proportions and decorations.'

Genoa morphed from a city of squalor. Dickens looked down upon its jumble of hills, streets and houses and no longer abhorred their disarray. 'There lies all Genoa, in beautiful confusion,' he wrote.

* * *

We arrived at Sanremo's ground in good time. We had an hour to spare before kick-off, and the plan was simple: park the car, find a bar, have a beer, then see what football's like down in Serie D. There was just one problem.

'There's no one here,' said John.

I didn't want John to be right. I'd been the organiser for this game. Sanremo v Imperia, strictly speaking not a Serie D clash but a Coppa Italia game between two clubs in Serie D. I'd checked online on the Sunday after our trip to Genoa. The words were unequivocal:

'Sanremese v Imperia.'

To every football fan in any corner of the world, the conclusion from seeing those words is that Sanremo is the home side.

I checked again on Monday.

But John was right. Now, on Wednesday, 22 September, the car park adjacent to Sanremese's ground, the Stadio Communale, was empty. We would later come to realise that, on matchdays, you can't even drive into it. Today, we could, but there was no one in sight. I got out of the car and peered through the fencing on to the pitch. No one. Nothing. *Niente*. Save, at the far end, a man on a sit-on lawn mower.

I looked online via my phone. Uncannily, the fixture was now displaying as Imperia v Sanremese.

Imperia was about half an hour away by car. John and I were in the early days of a podcast about football on the Mediterranean coastline, called, either pointedly or unimaginatively, *Footy on the Med*. We'd been a bit hit and miss so far, making elementary errors such as failing to turn on the recording equipment and not allowing enough time to get to games. Today, albeit this wasn't the most glamorous of matches on the Med, we were determined to get it right. And here we were, nice and early, only for the game to have been rearranged as an Imperia home fixture.

There was only one thing for it. We'd sprint to Imperia, a coastal town of 43,000 inhabitants which was approaching its centenary: it was created by Benito Mussolini on 21 October 1923 when he combined Porto Maurizio and Onegli (which lie on either side of the River Impero) as well as several nearby villages. We made it, or at least we thought we did, finding one remaining space in a car park near Imperia's Stadio Nino Ciccione and rushing to the first entrance we saw. This, for €5 apiece, took us to uncovered terracing behind the goal at the northern end of the ground.

Almost as soon as we arrived, Imperia scored. Some 50 fans next to us went wild. To a man (and they were all men), they were black-clad, with 'Ultras' or 'Ultra' adorning their T-shirts. As soon as we'd arrived, they'd greeted our appearance with suspicion. And the more they stared, the more it dawned on John and me that we'd opted to stand in the area reserved for Imperia's ultras.

We did not, though, look like ultras ourselves. With Irish heritage, John is fair-skinned and light-haired. He is very large and has a hefty frame. I'm smaller, at 5ft 9in, and although my complexion means I've been taken for a local along the Med, for this game I was wearing a linen shirt and looking distinctly less than ultra. Moreover, the previous day I'd had an injection in my right knee. Resting hadn't improved it and I'd had a partial meniscectomy a couple of months earlier. It resolved my inability to flex the knee, but I was still in a lot of pain. France, though, is nothing if not a highly medicalised nation, and I found myself prescribed various post-op therapies, including standing in a freezing cold chamber for three minutes once a week and having Platelet-Rich Plasma (PRP) treatment. I'm not sure any of them made any difference, but I do know one side effect of PRP injections is not feeling too clever on my feet. This sensation did not ameliorate my concern about the ultras.

We were out of place. The stares of the Imperia hardcore were intimidating. That there were almost as many armed police as ultras added to our apprehension. The goal was a happy distraction, but when play resumed the looks came our way again. Perhaps, if we'd stayed put and said, *'Ciao! Come stei oggi?'* we'd have made lifelong friends. On the other hand, 'How are you doing today?' seemed as likely to result in, 'Not good, because you two are here.' And so, trying not to look too sheepish, we explained to the men on the gate that we'd like to leave, thanks very much, and watch the game from the main stand, which, we could see, had a smattering of two wonderful things – women and children. They were bemused, explaining that we'd have to walk round the side of the stadium and pay to enter again.

For John and me, the outlay of another €5 was money well spent. We had a better view of the action, were spared hostile looks, and could also now observe Sanremese's ultras, who'd congregated on the terrace behind the goal at the southern end. Again, there were about 50 of them, though Sanremese's contingent chose to be topless. Both sets of fans sang, chanted and hurled abuse at each other and opposing players with unstinting conviction, stopping for nothing for the entirety of the match. Strangely, the Sanremese mob seemed happier, despite being a goal down throughout. At half-time, both sets of players left the ground, walking across a car park to a building that presumably housed the dressing rooms. John wandered off in search of a snack, returning empty-handed but with the revelation that using the facilities was 'like using the loo in someone's house'.

The sense of whimsy to the game was accentuated by the layout of the Stadio Nino Ciccione. It's listed as having a capacity of either 3,900 or 3,300, depending on what you read, but while its main stand and two terraced ends behind the goals are compact and functional, there is virtually nothing by way of seating or terracing on the eastern side. Instead, there is a stone wall some 20 feet in width, near the northern end, on which a clutch of fans were sitting, and many houses with perfect views of the pitch. Quite a few local residents had forgone whatever they'd usually be doing on this Wednesday afternoon to watch the game. Every now and then, a train would appear on a track above the northern terrace. I racked my brain and couldn't think of a ground anywhere which is closer to a railway line; not even St James Park in Exeter.

But the thought of Exeter made we wonder: could the Grecians' derby against Torquay United be billed as the English Riviera derby? Probably not. I'd need to check – just as I'd need to check the exact boundaries of the French and Italian rivieras. For now, though, the question was whether Imperia could hang on to their 1-0 lead. Sanremese's goalkeeper, Bologna-born Jacopo Malaguti, looked unfeasibly young – closer to the number on his shirt, 12, than his 18 years at the time of the game – but was relatively untroubled. Sanremese's forwards were a constant threat. Still, though, Imperia hung on, and the spoils of this Italian Riviera derby would be going to them. In the distant future lay the final of the Coppa Italia; perhaps even a final against last year's winners, Juventus, the Old Lady.

Bizarrely, the final whistle saw scenes of delight among the Sanremese fans. One of them was sufficiently irked by something said by an Imperia player as he left the field that he shook his fists and tried to scale the 30ft fence between terrace and grass, but his cohorts were brandishing their flags and singing as if it were they, not black-and-blue-shirted Imperia, who were heading to the next round. Suddenly, it hit me. John and I had arrived late. Had we missed a goal?

The question gnawed away as we left the Stadio Nino Ciccione. If anything, there were now even more police, and up a street to our left we could see a mass of black – Imperia's ultras, not looking best pleased. We turned to our right, made it to my car and left Imperia without further ado.

Did we over-react? Did some vestigial image of Mussolini enter our minds, substituting menace for mere theatre? Certainly, the endless shouts of 'vaffanculo', 'bastardo' and 'cazzo' were unmistakeable. Imperia's ultras hadn't exactly welcomed us with open arms. Sanremese's fence-climber, at the end of the game, looked as if he was ready to die for a cause that only he understood. Online footage soon appeared, revealing a stand-off between the two sets of fans when the Sanremese team bus arrived. Massed ranks of police kept them apart on a narrow street near the ground. Still, some of them contrived to bang their fists against the nearest shop doors and wire-grilled windows. Maybe Mediterranean football didn't always come with an inherent dollop of the benign.

Back home in Menton I kept an eye on QPR's cup game that night. It was a League Cup third-round home tie against Everton. After a 2-2 draw at full-time, the Rs ultimately prevailed in a remarkable 8-7 penalty shoot-out.

Scrolling around online amid the goals, I discovered that Imperia had produced a Nobel Prize-winner in Giulio Nata, a chemist. I also found there is a football club that has a train track even closer than Imperia's: if you find yourself in Slovakia, watching TJ Tatran Čierny Balog, you will encounter a steam train running right through the stadium, between the stand and pitch. But far more significant was the revelation that Sanremese v Imperia on Wednesday, 22 September 2021, a Coppa Italia clash originally listed as being in Sanremo but played in Imperia, had ended Imperia 1, Sanremese 2.

Sanremese took the lead in the 15th minute, at roughly the moment we'd left my car. Imperia equalised in the 18th minute – this was the goal we half-saw, arriving just as the ball landed in the back of the net. But then, on 19 minutes, Sanremese's number 11, Diego Vita, scored his second goal. John and I were walking around the outside of the Stadio Nino Ciccione when this happened. Even Sanremese's diehards, numbering as they did no more than 50, couldn't make enough noise for us to register that their team had scored. There was no signage of any kind in the ground. It was sunny. We were having an afternoon out on the Italian Riviera. We were content to enjoy a decent game, largely free of the dark arts of Italian gamesmanship. We didn't think to ask anyone if the score was not 1-0 to Imperia. We also didn't ask why the game had been switched at the last minute.

The trains went back and forth above the north end terrace. They, at least, were free of confusion.

4

October 2021

Fantastic Times

WE WERE Genoa-bound again, this time for Sampdoria
v Udinese on Sunday, 3 October 2021. It was an appealing
fixture, logistically as much as anything, so far as I was
concerned: a short stroll from my house on Avenue
Katherine Mansfield in Menton led to the Rue Webb-Ellis
and Menton-Garavan train station. A journey of perhaps
four minutes, by foot, during which I would always tell
myself to find out more about Webb-Ellis, the English
clergyman who supposedly invented rugby when he picked
up the ball and ran with it during a school football match.
I knew Webb-Ellis was buried in Menton, but that was it.
Why did he decide to pick up the ball instead of kick it?
Did he mean to create a new sport? Surely not. But was his
act one of bravery, or self-preservation? Had Webb-Ellis
gone on to delight in the sport he'd created and had he
even exported it here, to the south of France?

The short walk from my house to Menton-Garavan
station was a regular part of my life at this point, because

I was seeing medics in Nice for differing zeitgeisty treatments to rehabilitate my knee. But no matter how many times I wondered about Webb-Ellis, the time was never there. He seemed destined to remain a mystery.

Today, I was heading east, with a ten-minute train ride to Ventimiglia, the first town across the border in Italy. Time for a coffee in one of the hubbub of cafes near Ventimiglia station, then back in the hands of Trenitalia for the two-hour trip to Genova Piazza Principe. With me, *Italian Ways: On and Off the Rails from Milan to Palermo* by Tim Parks, thanks to which, among many other eccentricities, I found that Italians do not move once they are on escalators. Apparently, they cannot see the point. For them, the idea of keeping one side of an escalator free for those in a hurry, à la New York Metro and London Underground, is madness. As Parks has it, the Italian view is that if you want to walk, use the stairs.

I tested this at Genova Piazza Principe. There, the escalators are so diminished they are barely worthy of the name. But short though they are, Parks was right. Everyone using them stepped on and, whether on the left or the right, stopped. Within about three seconds it was time to get off again. Still, no one moved, determinedly planting their feet as if this brief respite from the act of walking would be as restorative as a blessing from the Pope.

Our train had been delayed and so this time, having been joined by Nav and two of his friends at Sanremo, John and I hopped in a taxi to get to the Stadio Luigi Ferraris. Nav's friends were from South Africa – like him, they were working on boats in Sanremo. Once in the taxi,

John lost no time in launching a surprising diplomatic initiative.

'You're from South Africa?'

That's right, said the two lads.

'Do you know that great *Spitting Image* song?'

The lads said they didn't.

John then launched into 'I've Never Met a Nice South African', with its first chorus:

No, he's never met a nice South African
And that's not bloody surprising, man
'Cause we're a bunch of arrogant bastards
Who hate black people.

I felt for the lads. One was in his early 20s, the other was just 19. They probably had little idea of how South Africa was perceived when *Spitting Image*, the great British satirical show, was in its heyday. But I couldn't help but smile. Peter Fluck, *Spitting Image*'s co-founder with Roger Law, is a good friend of mine. Now in his 80s, he works as an artist from a cliff-top house on The Lizard in Cornwall, with his wife Anne-Cécile de Bruyne, also an artist. Age has not mellowed his political views. I half-hoped John wouldn't carry on with his version of the song, and half-hoped he would. Peter would have smiled.

* * *

It was one of the best goals I have ever seen.

A few minutes after the midway point of the second half, Fabio Quagliarella, Sampdoria's captain and penalty-scorer in the 48th minute, played a sharp right-footed pass from centre midfield to the right-hand side of the pitch, into the path of the oncoming Antonio Candreva. Candreva, capped 54 times by Italy, controlled the ball with his right foot, taking the sting out of it, so that it bobbled invitingly in front of him. Then, with immaculate technique, he leaned his body slightly to the left, pulling his left, trailing arm back before smashing the ball with the outside of his right foot. It raced 25, perhaps 30, yards towards the goalkeeper's top left-hand corner, its pace and curling flight meaning that Udinese's former Leeds United keeper, Marco Silvestri, didn't have a hope in hell of making a save.

The Stadio Luigi Ferraris erupted. Candreva rushed to the touchline and was embraced by players and coaching staff alike. In the 69th minute of a tremendous, free-flowing game, he'd put Sampdoria 3-2 ahead with an unforgettable, world-class strike.

Nav shook his head in wonder. 'What a goal, what a goal, what a finish,' he said. 'He absolutely leathered it. Just perfect, one of those finishes you dream of.'

Candreva and Quagliarella had been Sampdoria's outstanding players throughout, but this, the seventh league game of the Serie A season, was expected to be a close-fought encounter, and so it proved. Just two points and three places separated the two sides, with Udinese 13th on seven points and Sampdoria 15th on five points. Both had patchy form, *La Samp* having lost 3-2 away to Juventus and, before that, suffering a 4-0 home humbling by league leaders Napoli. Udinese began the season well, picking up four wins out of five across all competitions, but had succumbed to a third consecutive defeat last time out when they lost 1-0 to Fiorentina.

On the way to the game, John, Nav and I settled on 1-1 as the likely result. The final score was 3-3 and, even in the final few minutes, both sides kept attacking. Neither would settle for seeing out the draw made possible when, in the 82nd minute, Fernando Forestieri bundled in a corner kick for Udinese.

Nav, a Birmingham City fan, was impressed, so too his two South African friends.

'They've been stuck on the boats for two years because of Covid, and haven't seen any football for ages,' said Nav. 'They're loving it, just over the moon. And what a game. There are no schmucks in this league, that's for sure. Both teams kept at it all the way through, putting in the effort, playing fast, attacking football. And the sound this stadium generates is just fantastic. Imagine the noise if it was packed.'

Nav was right. On the day, there were just 4,292 people inside the 36,536-capacity Stadio Luigi Ferraris. Only about 100 Udinese fans made it to the game. But the stadium somehow confines and then amplifies every noise, generating an irresistible cacophony as if Vittorio Gregotti (who redesigned the ground for the 1990 World Cup, hosted by Italy) was a magician of sound rather than an architect. Perhaps its role in Italia '90 helped boost Sampdoria, co-tenants with Genoa of the Stadio Luigi Ferraris since 1946, to the club's best league finish the following year: in 1991, Sampdoria won the *Scudetto*.

For nearly a decade starting in 1985, Sampdoria were one of Europe's top clubs. The Coppa Italia was theirs four times, in 1985, 1988, 1989 and 1994. They won the European Cup Winners' Cup in 1990, and, in

1992, reached the final of the European Cup, losing 1-0 to Barcelona after extra time. This was the era of Serie A dominance in Europe – across the two decades of the 1980s and 1990s, Italian clubs won 17 continental trophies – and British players featured on Italian team-sheets far more than they do today. Sampdoria seemed to lure more UK players than most. The club's roll call includes Trevor Francis (the UK's first million-pound player when he joined Nottingham Forest from Birmingham City in 1979), who described his four years from 1982 to 1986, 68 appearances and 17 goals for Sampdoria as 'fantastic times'.

With Francis in Sampdoria's 1985 Coppa Italia-winning season was Scottish international and Liverpool legend Graeme Souness, who left Anfield in 1984 and joined *La Samp* for £650,000. 'I went there and found it easy,' said Souness, who played 56 times for Sampdoria between 1984 and 1986, scoring eight times. England midfielder David Platt also enjoyed a successful stint with the club, playing 55 league games over two years in the mid-1990s under Sven-Göran Eriksson and winning the Coppa Italia in 1994.

Others didn't fare so well. None of Des Walker, Lee Sharpe and Danny Dichio are likely to recall their Sampdoria days as 'fantastic times', but, during half-time, I learnt that Udinese had an English connection, too. In 2001, fresh from leading FC Copenhagen to the Danish title, Roy Hodgson joined Udinese, though what lured him to the team from Udine, a small city in north-east Italy between the Adriatic sea and the Alps, now seems obscure. Some things, though, are certain: Udinese, or *Le Zebrette* ('the little zebras'), were founded in 1896 and have played continuously in Serie A since the 1995/96 season. Despite their fine showing against Sampdoria, with ex-Watford and Everton forward Gerard Deulofeu giving the home side a roasting in the first half, Udinese are not known for winning much, if anything. Principal honours are limited to the Prima Divisione title in 1930, the Anglo-Italian Cup 1978 and the UEFA Intertoto Cup 2000. Hodgson's time with the club was less than fantastic: he was sacked after six months, allegedly offering an enigmatic parting shot, 'I could have chosen a better club to come back to. It's an extremely strange club.' And if Antonio Di Natale, capped 42 times by Italy, is probably Udinese's most revered player – with a fine haul of 191 goals in 385 appearances – the most famous ever to wear the black and white striped shirts must be Zico.

When Brazil's 'White Pele' was set to ply his trade in Friuli in 1983, it was described by a local journalist as like 'fitting the engine of a Ferrari into a Volkswagen'. The Italian Football Federation (IFF) expressed no less consternation, but for financial reasons: they believed Zico's putative transfer to be too expensive for a foreign player. Nevertheless, Zico arrived on 15 June 1983, to be met by 5,000 enraptured Friulians at the airport, and made his debut two days later in a five-minute cameo in a friendly match against the Brazilian club he'd been with for the past 12 years, Flamengo. Outraged administrators at the IFF then tried to block his registration, prompting yet greater outrage from the Udinesi, who, on 4 July protested in the city centre with placards proclaiming, 'O Zico o Austria' – they would join Austria if they couldn't have Zico. The wrangling continued, but by the beginning of the season Arthur Antunes Coimbra was a fully fledged, official Udinese player, to the disappointment of AS Roma and AC Milan, who'd coveted him, and to the delight of north-east Italy's native Friulians: more than 26,000 new season tickets were sold by Udinese for the 1983/84 season.

Zico did not disappoint. He became a legend in his two seasons at the club, scoring 57 goals in 79 appearances. He didn't manage to propel his new club to a *Scudetto*, but the fans loved him; many years later, on a return visit, Zico would declare 'it's always a pleasure to be here'. By then, one assumes, he had got over the disappointment of his final home game for Udinese, on 12 May 1985. It pitted Brazil against Argentina: Zico, 32, against another gifted number ten, Napoli's 24-year-old Diego Maradona. Maradona scored with a superb free kick on four minutes. Soon afterwards, a Zico free kick led to the ball being scrambled into the net. The whole of Friuli went wild in the second half when the Brazilian slid the ball from another free kick to Luigi De Agostini, who hammered it home with his left boot. It was 2-1, but then, in the 88th minute, along came Maradona. All 5ft 5in of him angled high into the air, to beat the Udinese goalkeeper with a header after the ball came off the crossbar from an earlier effort.

But was it a header? Zico thought not. 'If you're an honest man, confess to the referee that you used your hand!' were his words to the Argentinian. The weight of opinion, thanks to endless television replays, was on his side. It was in this game that Maradona had successfully trialled his infamous 'Hand of God'.

Zico's fury – he lost no time in letting the referee, Giancarlo Pirandola, know what he thought – only endeared him all the more to the Udinesi.

To think: they'd been prepared to secede to another country if they couldn't have him.

* * *

Two of the hardest, most granite-jawed and all-round terrifying men I've ever seen came sprinting past us. They looked ready to kill. Profanities flew from their mouths and the sinews on their ripped arms and necks rippled as their eyes, frigid and stony like an assassin's, targeted the mid-point of Stadio Comunale's south-facing stand. For a second, as they rushed towards us, John and I thought we were their prey. But no. It was the halfway line. Specifically, the 15ft fence separating Sanremese's fans from the pitch at the halfway line.

They flung themselves at it and started to climb. *'Bastardo!'* they cried. *'Cazzo!' 'Vaffanculo!'* The object of their ire, the game's referee, was unperturbed. So, too, Casale's players. Now the men started to rock back and forth on the fence, eyes glazed with rage. *'Bastardo! Vaffanculo!'* Still their anger met with no reaction – on the pitch, at least. Behind them, some 15 to 20 Sanremese ultras poured fuel on the fire. I am not sure of their exact words, but the sentiment was very much along the lines of the English refrain, 'The referee's a wanker!' No one on the pitch paid them any attention. Other fans began to trudge out of the ground. John and I weren't so tardy. We didn't fancy running into the two ringleaders. They were cartoon caricature hard men: perhaps 40 years old, not an ounce of fat on their bodies, all pumped-up muscle heaving against tight T-shirts, faces as etched with angular lines as the characters of *Sin City*.

Bumping into this pair, as two English blokes along for a nice afternoon's football, was of no appeal at all. To run would have attracted attention. Let's just say we impersonated a couple of Olympic walkers as we made a beeline for the exit and, beyond it, the safety of Sanremo's seafront.

There, the sun had given way to a scattering of clouds. The surf had dropped off and the surfers had gone home. Sanremese had just lost 2-1 to Casale. Their afternoon had taken a turn for the worse in the 36th minute, when 20-year-old midfielder Diego La Rotunda had been sent off for collecting a second yellow card. Nevertheless, playing neat, passing football, they'd got to the interval at 0-0 and then taken the lead in the 69th minute thanks to a goal by Filippo Dadone. Their goalkeeper, Malaguti – who'd made his debut in the game at Imperia – was having a blinder, saving a penalty in the first half and seeming to deny Casale at will. An improbable victory was not to be, thanks mainly to a Frenchman from Nice, who, for a while, had played in the bitter cold of north-east England. Step forward Malaury Martin, formerly of Middlesbrough. He'd looked classy throughout, pulling the strings alongside the Casale number ten, Roberto Candido, before scoring with a right-footed drive in the 79th minute. Four minutes later, Candido made it 2-1 to the away side. Sanremese scored again in the final moments, only for the goal to be disallowed.

At half-time, we'd got talking to a couple of Casale fans. Gianluca and Roberto were a journalist and photographer, who, they said, happened to be working in Sanremo rather than being there solely to support their team. They were curious about John and me. 'You look like you're from the Mediterranean,' said Gianluca to me. Then, gesturing to John, he said, 'But he doesn't.' Then he got to the point, 'What are you doing here?' We explained we were putting together a podcast, and that I was researching a book. They were generous on the back of Italy's Euro 2020 triumph over England. 'Italy deserved to win it, though maybe the French would disagree,' said Gianluca. 'But why is England always so good before every tournament, but doesn't ever win anything?' There was a range of possible answers, but soon Roberto posed another question. 'How can a team with Steven Gerrard, Wayne Rooney and Frank Lampard not win a title?' Again, a shake of the head seemed the only reasonable response.

I asked about my belief – given some impetus by the sight of the surfers in the sea, the blue of the Mediterranean, Sanremo's genteel streets, and the sheer gorgeousness of the weather – that football on the Med might be that bit more chilled than elsewhere, somehow influenced and affected by the gentler rhythms of life in so favoured a climate and landscape.

Gianluca didn't agree, 'Football is football, wherever you are. It's the same. Maybe faster in the Premier League, but the same.'

Gianluca suggested I ask Malaury Martin for his thoughts, 'He played in the Premier League, he would know if it is different.'

That was a good idea. Martin, 33, had signed for newly promoted Blackpool in August 2010 and, although he didn't feature in their 2010/11 campaign, he'd played 15 times for Championship side Middlesbrough the following season. Beginning his career with AS Monaco, Martin, a midfielder who'd represented France at six levels up to the Under-21s, had played for clubs in France, Italy, Switzerland, Norway and Scotland. He'd even had a trial in the United States, with Major League Soccer side Chicago Fire. If anyone would have an authoritative view on Mediterranean football and whether it's any different to football elsewhere, it would be this much-travelled son of the French Riviera, who was born in Nice in 1988. And, with the Stadio Communale being so intimate, it didn't seem out of the question to hang around and snag a chat with Martin just as the Casale players would be leaving.

But the men with the granite jaws scotched the idea. As John and I moved quickly but, we hoped, unobtrusively, past the enraged Sanremese fans, I noted Gianluca and Roberto doing the same. This wasn't the time or place to nail one's colours to the Casale mast.

5

October 2021

Savanier's Spells

MONTPELLIER IS not on the French Riviera. I wasn't
sure if it was, but while checking whether Torquay United v
Exeter City could properly be billed as 'the English Riviera
derby' (it can't), I also double-checked the boundaries of
the French Riviera. There is no official demarcation, but
it seems the Riviera is generally regarded as running along
the coast from Toulon, Saint-Tropez or Hyères in the west
to Menton in the south-eastern corner of France. That
put Montpellier some way from the French Riviera – a
solid two and a half-hour drive from Toulon – and I was
further confounded by the discovery that the city is not
on the Mediterranean itself, lying some six miles inland.

But during a short break in the Occitaine town of
Meze, I realised that Montpellier HSC would be at home
to Lens. Meze was 40 minutes by car from Montpellier.
Laurent Blanc, Eric Cantona and Olivier Giroud were
just three of an impressive roll call of former players for a
club that was a founder member, in 1932, of the French

first division. Montpellier, along with Marseille, Rennes and Nice, were one of the only teams that had played continually in the top tier. They'd won the Ligue 1 title in 2011/12, and the Coupe de France twice, in 1929 and 1990. There was yet more glamour: World Cup stars Roger Milla and Carlos Valderrama had also been Montpellier players. And, in the form of 23-year-old striker Stephy Mavididi, Montpellier had that very rare thing: an English professional footballer making his living on the continent.

An outing to Montpellier's stadium, the Stade de la Mosson, was a must.

* * *

'Lens will win 1-0.' This was the prediction of Eric Prada, a friend from Menton. Caroline, Maud and I were staying with Eric, his wife Lydie and their son Emilio in Meze, a fishing town on the Via Domitia, the ancient Roman road linking Italy, France and Spain. Hailing originally from Lyon and a Menton resident for the past few years, Eric's forecast was grounded in an objective appraisal of the two teams' recent form (as would also befit a man who works as an automotive racing data analyst): coming into the match, Racing Club de Lens were yet to lose and were second in Ligue 1. In contrast, Montpellier Hérault Sport Club hadn't won in their past four games. Their patchy form saw them occupy a lacklustre 13th place in the table.

Thanks to Eric, I had a match programme. None had been available at any of the games I'd seen so far. This would remain a feature of Mediterranean football for the whole season. Whether in Italy or France, a programme was as rare as a white peacock. In Spain and Greece, it was the same. I'd have better luck asking for directions to the nearest ski shop. Go to any English game and there's always a programme to be had. They're sold at almost every entry point to the ground. Not so on the Med. Not once did I find anyone selling any.

At Nice's Allianz Riviera stadium, I got hold of a programme for each of the four games I attended, but only because they'd been discarded and were being trampled into the concrete, either as I was arriving or leaving. Likewise, along the coast at the Stade Louis II. I went to a few AS Monaco matches, but the only one blessed by a programme was by accident. It was on the floor bisecting the doorway of the gents, at half-time. The occasion was the visit of Paris Saint-Germain. The programme's whereabouts was either apposite, or appalling. Everywhere else, nothing. No evidence that a programme had even been printed, let alone was for sale.

Of course, English naivety may explain all this. Perhaps clubs along the Med had seen the environmental light, and announced years ago they'd not be bothering with antediluvian paper anymore, 'No, not for us, we've gone digital, don't you know, besides, who among the younger generation, our future livelihood, reads anything anywhere anymore, unless it's on their phone?' Or maybe programmes weren't part of their culture, so that OGC Nice and AS Monaco were pioneers, early adoptees of a decades-old but just-unearthed English tradition. Or, possibly, programmes were printed and sold, but only for season ticket-holders who received them in the post, then brought them to games and hurled them to the floor, disgusted at their club's insistence on old-school media.

Or, conceivably, programmes were available at every *other* entrance to those I used, randomly and with no forethought, because sometimes life is random and unplanned.

Save, though, for this balmy Sunday afternoon on 17 October 2021, when Eric brandished a programme as if it came out of thin air.

'Where did you get it?' I asked.

'A lady gave me two,' said Eric.

Eric is a charming, handsome man. Perhaps this had something to do with it. Either way, it was a relief to flick through a programme and see the teams' line-ups, rather than peer downwards into my phone. Whoever had written the programme was also spot-on in identifying Lens midfielder Seko 'omniprésent' Fofana as a player to watch. Marseille-born Valère Germain was also profiled, and had a good game. But the result of this clash ultimately came down to two men: erstwhile Arsenal junior Mavididi, and Montpellier local Téji Savanier.

Mavididi signalled his intent from the start. Wearing the number ten shirt and played in by Germain, Mavididi cut inside from just outside the left-hand edge of the penalty box and confused two Lens defenders enough to find space and clip a smart, low and curling right-foot shot to the goalkeeper's left. It went fractionally wide. Shortly afterwards, Savanier sent in a low cross from the left, to be hit against the post, this time by Germain. The game ebbed and flowed at pace, Savanier at the heart of everything for *La Paillade,* so called because Montpellier HSC is in a neighbourhood of the same name. He was popular, too.

The Stade de la Mosson, used in the 1998 Fifa World Cup, was some way from being full to its 32,900 capacity, but a healthy number had made the long trek from northern France to support *Le sang et or* ('the blood and gold', the colour of Lens shirts) and helped make this a boisterous crowd of 12,474. But the majority in the ground were rhapsodic about Savanier. His Wikipedia entry has him as still living with his parents in Figuerolles, a district in Montpellier, but anyone inferring that this betrays some form of immaturity would be wrong. Savanier played with extraordinary verve and élan, captaining Montpellier with all the authority of *Le président* himself – Laurent Blanc, who made 243 appearances for the club.

Three minutes into the second half, it was a pass from Savanier that unlocked the Lens defence. Struck with his right foot from just inside his own half, Savanier's ball bisected two retreating Lens players to slide perfectly into the path of Mavididi. The Englishman's timing was immaculate, both in his run to stay onside and his finish – a cool-headed, low shot to the goalkeeper's left, for his third goal of the season.

The Stade de la Mosson erupted. In front of us, a collective of six fans was especially ecstatic. Neither Eric nor I had seen Montpellier's innovation anywhere else in football – three pitchside sofas, set just a couple of feet from the touchline. In front of each was a sheet of see-through Perspex (I assume it was Perspex), presumably to protect the fans from too robust a clearance or any Cantona-esque balletics. The sofa had room for two spectators. To a man, they leapt from the comfort of their repose, punching the air in praise of Savanier and Mavididi. One, wearing a

Savanier shirt, seemed so euphoric it was as if his hero had scored for him alone.

Savanier continued to deliver, but so too did Fofana. Born in France but an Ivory Coast international – in April 2017, Fofana chose to represent the country of his parents' birth, having represented France at Under-16, Under-17, under-18 and under-19 levels – Fofana put in a towering second-half display. He was strong, quick and skilful, and set about trying to power Lens on to the scoresheet. But even in the dying minutes, when Montpellier's Jordan Ferri was sent off for a second yellow-card offence (a discreet but discernible tug on Fofana's shirt as he charged through midfield), Fofana and Lens couldn't quite take the game from the tireless Savanier, who almost got the goal he deserved with a viciously curling and dipping shot from outside the box in the 86th minute. Jean-Louis Leca's save wasn't the most comfortable, but he kept the score at 1-0 to the home side.

And there it ended. Montpellier's manager, Oliver Dall'Oglio, a defender who'd left Brest to take the helm in June, seemed as relieved as he was happy. In a game in which possession was split 50/50, that was fair enough. Savanier was all smiles, as was Mavididi, and I felt a strange sense of pride in this English number ten, a man who was the same age as my younger son. Here he was, Derby-born, making a name for himself on the Med and in Ligue 1. Mavididi began his career at Southend United before joining Arsenal at the age of 13. He didn't make any senior appearances for Arsenal but did play for Charlton and Preston on loan and, in June 2020, he joined Montpellier in a €6m deal. He'd been a Juventus player too, making one senior appearance with the titans of modern Italian football in a 2-1 away defeat, in April 2019, to Ferrara club SPAL. In making that appearance, Mavididi became the first English player since David Platt in 1992 to play for the Old Lady.

Walking away from the Stade de la Mosson, to drive back to Meze for a meal with Lydie's parents, I realised my conceit – that the experience of football along the Mediterranean coastline might somehow be more genial than elsewhere – had just had a massive shot in the arm. It had been a great afternoon's football, under the sun and a clear blue sky. Stephy Mavididi, one of the handful of English footballers playing on the continent, had got the game's only goal. Savanier had been a revelation. I'd never heard of him before the game; he was bewitching to watch. Fofana was brilliant too. The fans were passionate but not aggressive. The quality of football was very high; the ball was never hoofed up in the air, and both sets of players always looked to play a fast, intricate passing game. Why, Montpellier HSC even had a hooped theme going on – well, thin orange lines set horizontally against their blue shirts, at least.

Montpellier HSC v Racing Club de Lens, which kicked off at 3pm on Sunday, 17 October 2021, turned out to be the best 1-0 game I've ever seen.

6

November 2021

Football Can Be a Game of One Half

IT ALL seemed simple enough. Leave Menton at 3pm on Sunday, 7 November. Drive the 30 minutes to Nice airport, arriving nice and early. Park, wait, do some French on Duolingo. Wave to John as he emerges from Terminal 2, fresh as a daisy after a short flight from Paris, due in at 3.45pm. Amaze him with a new French phrase or two as we drive the ten minutes to the Allianz Riviera, home of four-time Ligue 1 winners Olympique Gymnaste Club Nice Côte d'Azur. Park the car, walk to the ground well before the 5pm kick-off, take our seats, watch Nice play Montpellier. Drive home to Menton. A nice and easy afternoon out to see some footy on the Med.

The first part went to plan. I made good time driving to the airport along the A8 autoroute, the highway – also known as *La Provençale* – which links Aix-en-Provence with several towns on the Côte d'Azur before becoming the A10 when it reaches Italy. Menton to Nice is a fine drive, with views of pretty hillside villages such as Castellar and Gorbio as well as the sea far below between Menton and Monaco.

I'd had a heavy week of work and Caroline and I had had a couple of testy debates on what had become a perennial topic: should we stay in France for longer than our planned two years, or call it quits and return to England? Caroline was keen on the latter. Covid had put paid to my words of reassurance before we came to France. 'It's just 90 minutes by plane to Bristol, cheap on easyJet too, we can be home to see family in no time,' I'd said, only to find that travel became nigh-on impossible. Caroline badly missed her father and her brother, the rest of her family too. She was worried Covid would return, marooning us once again miles from home. She felt our two-year adventure should remain exactly that. I felt the opposite.

I was smitten. Life in France, so close to Italy, was fantastic. Our daughter was now fluent in French. I loved our morning routine on weekdays, lifting Maud into the seat on the back of our pushbike and then cycling along the pavement abutting Porte de France, the sea to our left, the soft yellows, pinks and ochres of Menton's Old Town sparkling in the sun ahead of us. I'd leave the bike beside the *escaliers* on Rue Longue and we'd climb the steps, to walk past the 17th-century Basilica of Saint-Michel and then on to École Adrien Camaret on Montée du Souvenir. I'd lose count of the number of '*bonjours*' and '*ca vas?*' en route: the French insist on politeness from an early age, and each child, as much as their parents, was expected to acknowledge the likes of Doumé and his wife Cécile, two Italian film-makers we'd befriended called Carlo and

Francesca, Luciano, an architect, and his American wife Holly, Eric and Lydie, Karolina from the Czech Republic, Adeline or her husband Thomas, Roxanna and Eric from Romania, who ran the Casi Dali restaurant on Quai Bonaparte – anyone and everyone, it seemed.

Once Maud was in school, the ritual would be repeated on the way back down to the bike, but often I'd find time to stand on the mosaic square in front of the basilica, to gaze at the sea and the mountains on the frontier of France and Italy. The view was breathtaking. I couldn't believe our luck in living here. I'd cycle back along Avenue Porte de France and pop into L'Amie du Pain for a coffee and to pick up our daily bread. Vincent, Blondine and Christel had got used to us now; on Saturdays and Sundays, we'd go there as a family, and they'd always make a fuss of Maud.

Living on Avenue Katherine Mansfield in Garavan, we were close enough to the bustle of Old Town and yet separate, with the sea just a few minutes' walk and any number of quiet *sentiers* leading to and from the elegant Boulevard de Garavan. I still hadn't got round to reading any Mansfield, but I knew of one line written by the New Zealand writer, who, in 1920/21, had lived in the house opposite ours, Villa Isola Bella. 'Menton is a lovely little town, small and unreal,' she wrote, adding, 'its colour and movement … make you continually happy'.

I missed my family, my sons Harry and Elliot, my parents, my brother Chris and his wife Emily, my sister Suki, their respective children; I missed Cornwall and all our friends there too. I missed Caroline's family, just as she missed mine. But I'd very rarely been as happy, anywhere, as I was in Menton, and when I put everything on a pair of scales, life on the Med was the winner. I understood Caroline's feelings. Of course I did. I respected them and empathised. But perhaps the blind faith inculcated by virtue of being a QPR fan played a part in my thinking. Covid wouldn't come back. Or, if it did, it'd be a lesser strain. The world would adjust. We'd all adjust. We'd be able to hop on a plane and get home to see our nearest and dearest with ease. Why, now that travel was possible again, maybe we'd even see more of everyone than before? Let's face it: Penzance isn't the most conveniently located town in England.

This discussion would pop up from time to time, a surefire trespasser on tranquillity. But, as usual, we'd park it without resolution. After all, it was only November, and we had another eight months to go in our rented house.

The previous day, we had a lovely walk in the Italian village of Villatella, a few miles inland over the border. We'd often head that way, to walk the dogs in the hills beyond Mortola de Superiore, Grimaldi, Seazla or further afield to the villages north of Dolceaqua. We'd find deserted churches, deep forests, mountain paths, rivers and streams and, at Villatella, a waterfall. The weekend was doing what weekends are supposed to do. The stress had waned. As I drove along the A8, I told myself to relax. The lockdown-driven stop-start of our first year in France was over. I'd seen some great football, we were getting out and about as a family again. I needed to chill. Life was good. *Que sera, sera.*

With these amiable sentiments I parked in Nice airport's unusually busy pick-up area. I wasn't just on time, I was early. I opened the Duolingo app and went through an exercise on sensations, which included the question '*es-tu stressé?*' *Pas du tout*, I thought, *je suis très content.*

The minutes ticked by. I dipped in a book about Alexandre Dumas, author of *The Three Musketeers* and *The Count of Monte Cristo*. Dumas had stayed in Nice in 1835. He encountered a group of travelling English women. They did not captivate him. *Les Anglaises* were 'pale, frail women without the strength to live elsewhere, who come to Nice each winter to die'. A tad harsh, I felt, but no less vehement was the English novelist Graham Greene, who lived a few miles along the coast in Antibes from 1966 until his death in 1991. It's fair to say Greene did not like Nice. In *J'Accuse* (1982), he savaged the city as being run by the mafia, cautioning anyone tempted to settle there, 'Avoid the region of Nice which is the preserve of some of the most criminal organisations in the south of France: they deal in drugs, they have attempted with the connivance of high authorities to take over the casinos.'

I'd barely visited Nice, thanks to Covid restrictions. The trips I'd made had almost all been to its medical establishments, which are mainly clustered in the hilltop residential suburb of Cimiez. I was excited, at last, to be going to the Allianz Riviera, a stadium I'd often driven past on *La Provençale*. I'd get to see Téji Savanier, Montpellier's brilliant ball-player, again, as well as Mavididi and a much-feted Nice player called Amine Gouiri. OGC Nice even had an eagle called Mèfi, who, according to the club website, 'kickstarts every home game by flying into the stadium'. So, Graham Greene, away with you. I was up for this match. Nothing was going to dent my mood.

But the clock ticked on. There was no sign of John. At this rate, it might be a scramble to get to the ground and park in time. I checked the team line-ups on my phone. There would be no Savanier; he was suspended. Still no sign of John until, praise be, a text message. 'The flight was delayed but I've landed!' it said. Another message followed instantly. 'Trouble is they haven't got one of those connecting things so we can disembark.'

I believe the technical term is a jetbridge. To wait for it, or press on to the game? This was slated to be another podcast in our *Footy on the Med* series. If I went ahead alone, at least I could record some audio into my phone.

I opted to wait. John's messages were not reassuring. 'There's no sign of it yet.' 'Still sitting here.' 'Still nothing.'

Finally, we made the call: I'd drive on to the Allianz Riviera on my own.

Nice's airport pick-up zone was now heaving with cars. I edged as quickly as I could through the traffic and headed for the A8, not bothering with Google Maps because the route was simple. It was 4.45pm, but it'd only take about eight minutes, and if I was lucky, and found a place to park, I'd only miss a few minutes of the game.

If waiting optimistically for John's jetbridge was my first mistake, not bothering with Google Maps was the second. Driving too fast, and assuming the route was easy when I'd never done it before, I plumped for the first right turn I found once on the A8. It had to be for the Allianz Riviera, surely?

Surely not. The road wended away to the west and then went due north. There was nowhere to turn round, no roads off it. The first sign I saw told me I was driving to Lantosque.

I like Lantosque. Caroline, Maud and I had a weekend away in the nearby, precipitous village of Saint Colomban during one of the lockdown lulls, when travel was possible. But I had absolutely no desire to be heading that way again, at what was now gone kick-off.

I drove on and on. Finally there was a turning to the right. I flung the car into it and sped back towards Nice. There, before me, was the Allianz Riviera. My muttered curses turned to pleas. *Please let me get this bit right and find a parking space.*

I got it wrong. Somehow, and to this day I have no idea how, I ended up back on the A8, pointing east. Menton, said the sign. I swore. Then I swore again. I swore more and more violently. No! I love Menton but no! I don't want to be driving back there now! What a cock-up.

It was 5.30pm by the time I found an exit and doubled back to the Allianz Riviera. *Drive slowly*, I said to myself. *Don't fuck this up as well.* But slowly though I drove, there was no getting through the police blockade preventing access to the stadium's main parking area. What now? I shimmied through a small gap in a barrier into a side road. Cars were parked in every available space, until, miracle of miracles, a man got into his VW and gestured to me that he was leaving. I parked, jumped out of the car and ran to the ground. It took about five minutes. I arrived just as half-time was beginning.

I had missed the whole of the first half. All of the past week's stress came back, and, for a moment, I wanted to cry. But lo, as I wearily looked for my seat, there was John.

'Great to see you, man!' he boomed, slapping me on the shoulder. 'But are you OK? What's wrong?'

My voice hoarse from so much swearing, I told him I'd buy some beers and then tell him what had happened. I'd seldom felt the need for a beer so intensely. They were non-alcoholic, but I didn't care. I went to get my wallet to pay. And then I realised: in my haste I'd left it on the dashboard. I could see it there, a brazen invitation to any of Graham Greene's passing criminals.

'I can't believe it,' said John. 'I got here before you!'

It was true. As soon as he could, John had jumped in a cab. His driver was sympathetic, speeding swiftly to the Allianz Riviera. John made it just as the first half was ending.

'It's 0-0,' he said, as we sat down. 'I don't think we've missed much.'

We'd missed Mèfi the eagle, and, as the second half got under way, Montpellier were missing Savanier. They'd come into the game with a poor record against Nice, having lost their past five Ligue 1 games at the Allianz Riviera. Now, without Savanier, they were struggling. Nice, third in Ligue 1, were purposeful. A driving run by midfielder Lucas Da Cunha, receiving the ball in his own half, exemplified their dominance. Having covered almost half the pitch Da Cunha hit a powerful, low, left-footed shot, which Montpellier's keeper, Switzerland international Jonas Omlin, did well to push past the post. Next it was Mario Lemina's turn. The Gabonese international, who'd had spells with Marseille, Juventus, Southampton and Fulham, deftly controlled the ball, turned his man and hit the crossbar. It was all Nice, to the delight of most of

the 20,157 crowd, but, in the 80th minute Montpellier
threw a sucker punch. A quick counter-attack on the left
wing culminated in a teasing cross by Serbian international
Mihailo Ristić, which seemed to bounce off Mavididi into
the path of Florent Mollet. A seasoned midfielder, Mollet
hit a perfect left-footed drive into the bottom-left corner
of the goal. Nice pressed, but couldn't find an equaliser
and it ended in a 1-0 win for the away side. *La Paillade*'s
manager, Olivier Dall'Oglio, wore the look of a man
who'd just witnessed a successful daylight robbery.

The last time Montpellier won at the Allianz Riviera,
thanks to a last-minute Olivier Giroud goal, they bagged
their sole Ligue 1 title. I didn't fancy them to repeat their
2011/12 triumph, but they were a decent side and, with
Savanier back, who knows? Perhaps they were in with a
shout for Europe.

The thought of my wallet on the car dashboard
interrupted our post-match chat. One of the few
things I recall was John asking me if Nîmes was on the
Mediterranean. 'Yes, of course it is,' I said. John suggested
we take our families for a weekend in Nimes, and launched
into a tale about the origin of denim; the fabric of the jeans
we all wear apparently comes from Nîmes. I tugged at his
sleeve. 'My wallet,' I said.

It was still there. None of Greene's Niçois criminals
had chanced upon it. Perhaps they no longer exist. But if
OGC Nice v Montpellier HSC had defied the football
cliché – for us, it proved football could be a game of one
half, not two – my conviction that I know my map was
similarly upended when we worked out the logistics for
a Ligue 2 clash between Nîmes and Union Sportive

Quevillaise-Rouen Métropole, a team from Le Petit-Quevilly in northern France whose name, thankfully, is generally commuted to QRM.

Nîmes, dubbed by *The Telegraph* as 'the most Roman city outside Italy', is not on the Mediterranean.

We went all the same. So few outings had happened during our first year in France; seeing another part of the country was irresistible. Besides, Nîmes wasn't *that* far from the sea (40km, as the crow flies) and *Les Crocodiles*, as the city's football team are known, may be a resolutely second division club (very few forays below or above Ligue 2 have occurred), but they can lay claim to having had international stars of serious calibre on their books: think Laurent Blanc and Eric Cantona, the latter having joined Leeds United on loan from Nîmes in 1992.

I'd seen Cantona play against QPR when he was a Manchester United player. He was outstanding. And implacable. He played as if he was preordained to score, the most hurtful memory of which was the visit of United to Loftus Road on 16 March 1996. I was one of the 18,817 urging QPR on to what would have been a famous victory. We were ahead thanks to a Danny Dichio shot that Denis Irwin headed into his own net. Dichio may not have fared well at Sampdoria, but he was our hero that day. Then Robbie Hart, the referee, decided to add what felt like 15 minutes of stoppage time. Up popped Cantona to head home. The final score was 1-1. QPR were relegated from the Premier League by the end of the season. If we'd held on to the win, it wouldn't have been enough, points-wise, to keep us up. But what a boost if we'd beaten Manchester United! A lot of QPR fans, myself included, believe it was Cantona's injury-time equaliser that sealed our fate.

I'd seen another former Nîmes player too. Malaury Martin, so influential for Casale in their game against Sanremese at the Stadio Comunale, played for Nîmes on loan in the 2008/09 season.

There was also another, less tenuous link to QPR. Scottish midfielder, Andrew Wilson, left Chelsea in 1931 to play 20 times for the Rs, scoring three goals, before joining Nîmes in 1932. He returned to the UK for a brief spell as manager of Walsall and, in 1945, he reached the finals of the lawn bowls men's triples at the National Championships.

Lawn bowls, so quintessentially English; Nîmes, for all its Roman heritage, is classically French. Caroline put it well when we met John, Helén and their two children, Ben and Esmé, for lunch in the Old Town on Saturday. 'Welcome to France,' she said.

Everything about Nîmes is picture-postcard France. We stayed in a hotel opposite Les Arènes, one of France's best-preserved amphitheatres, and couldn't believe the beauty of the place. Roman architecture sets the tone, from the amphitheatre and immaculate Maison Carrée to the Romanesque frieze on the cathedral and the classical restraint of the Jardin de la Fontaine. But it's the maze of the Old Town that makes Nîmes so French. Brasseries, restaurants, intertwining alleyways, shops of all kinds, a throng of people at every turn and, in the Place du Marché, a life-sized crocodile in a fountain. Crocodiles abound, generally, whether as souvenirs, studs in pavements or on doorways, the reason apparently being because the first coin minted in Nîmes featured a crocodile chained to a palm frond on one side. The crocodile symbolised Egypt, vanquished in the Battle of Actium in 31BC, while the palm represented victory. François I made the crocodile the official emblem of Nîmes when he awarded the city a new coat of arms in 1535.

The footballing crocodiles' home is the Stade des Costières, a hike of some 30 minutes from Les Arènes. It's an impressive ground, with two covered stands pitchside and uncovered terracing behind each goal, and it looks as if it should hold more than its 18,482 capacity. The record attendance for the stadium, which was designed by Vittorio Gregotti (of Stadio Luigi Ferraris fame), is 25,051, this for Nîmes Olympique v Marseille in the 1991/92 season.

Nowhere near that number turned up for the 7pm kick-off on Saturday, 20 November. John and I were two of just 1,203, a long way from the average home gate of 7,288. It was a cold November night, but the fans weren't deterred by the weather. Instead, they'd decided to boycott the game by way of protest against the owner of the club, Beirut-born Rani Assaf. Earlier in the week, Nîmes' supporters had hosted a press conference at the Brasserie des Costières, in which they agreed to steer clear of the QRM fixture because of their belief that Assaf, one of the richest men in France with a fortune estimated at €112m, would somehow run the club into nothingness. Assaf had taken control of Nîmes in 2016 and, in the short time available after we'd taken the kids around Les Arènes, I'd managed to discover that things had been fractious ever since. There seemed to be problem after problem, controversy after controversy, and now it seemed that even

Jean-Paul Fournier, the mayor of Nîmes, had had enough. Everything I read, via Google searches on my phone, was in French, but in a bid to improve our language skills Caroline and I had recently watched *Le Mépris*, the 1963 Jean-Luc Godard film starring Brigitte Bardot. There was that word – *mépris* – again, in a statement by Fournier:

'*Tous ensemble, nous avons pu partager notre opposition à la politique sportive menée par le président Assaf. Les spectateurs des matchs de Nîmes Olympique méritent le respect. Je n'accepte plus le mépris de M. Assaf envers les supporters et les Nîmois.*'

What that meant, even to me with my less than fluent French, was clear. The mayor of Nîmes had met the diehards of *Les Crocodiles*. He'd listened to their woes. He sympathised. And he wouldn't accept the contempt – *le mépris* – of Assaf any more.

QRM didn't seem to have any sympathy with whatever ailed Nîmes Olympique. The small club from Normandy started well in this, a mid-table Ligue 2 clash. Yet again, I was struck by how rarely either side hoofed the ball. Even under pressure, players wanted to play. QRM had the edge and took the lead in the 16th minute thanks to Duckens Nazon, a Haitian international who'd had spells in the UK with Wolves, Coventry City, Oldham Athletic and St Mirren. Nazon was first to react to a shot that came off the post, side-footing home with ease. Nîmes countered in a watchable game that was probably at lower Championship level, Icelandic striker Elías Már Ómarsson equalising five minutes before half-time with a clever back-heel into the net. Again QRM came at the hosts, but in the 54th minute Yassine Benrahou, a 22-year-old €1.5m signing from Bordeaux in the summer of 2020, scored what would be the game's winner with a header. Try as they might, QRM, losing finalists in the Coupe de France in 1927 and 2012, couldn't get back on even terms.

The game began to peter out. John made a call for an early exit. It wasn't that we had to beat the crowd – there wasn't one. But it was cold, and we had a half-hour walk back to the Old Town, and if we left just a little bit early we'd be sure of getting a table in a restaurant. Good points, all, but my immediate response was no, we couldn't go early. It wasn't the done thing.

'Have you never, ever left a game early, then?' asked John.

And then I remembered. I'd not only left early, I'd left at half-time. It was at Middlesbrough v QPR on 20 November 2015. Six years to the day of Nîmes v QRM. I was in the north-east to take my son Elliot, then in the middle of his A-levels, to Durham University. By coincidence, or discreet planning, I realised that QPR would be playing at the Riverside Stadium on the evening of Friday, 20 November. I'd never been to the Riverside, and would always go to a QPR game if there was one to be seen. Luckily, Elliot and Caroline agreed to come too. The game was irredeemably dull. We might as well have gone to the Arctic. It was freezing. As a fan, the cold is OK. Of course I can accept it. I could even have sat through the whole of QPR's drab defensive display and felt happy if we'd come away with the 0-0 draw we were playing for. But at half-time I looked at Elliot and Caroline. Both like football. Elliot can play the game well. Caroline has been to a lot of QPR games with me over the years. But neither is a real, or even occasional, football fan. Elliot was shivering. Caroline was turning blue. I wavered, but decided: I couldn't do this to them. I couldn't make them slip into hypothermia at the Riverside, for the abstract (for them) notion of Queens Park Rangers FC.

Back in our Durham hotel, I found the highlights on TV. QPR had clung on to 0-0 until the 93rd minute, when they'd conceded a penalty. Grant Leadbitter stepped up and put it away.

To think: I could have persuaded Elliot and Caroline to endure the second half. We'd have got all the way to virtually the last kick of an action-free, desperately tedious game, only to see QPR lose. By then, they'd have frozen to near death.

John and I stayed to the end of Nîmes v QRM. It was cold, but not as cold as that night on the Riverside.

* * *

The burr of English was unexpected. At first, I thought I must be imagining it, but, craning my neck backwards, there was no doubt. I stole a quick look and sure enough, a few rows behind there was a group of Englishmen. Perhaps five or six, mainly dressed in black and in their mid-to-late 20s. All speaking in unmistakable midland accents.

This was AS Monaco, *Les Rouges et Blancs,* v Real Sociedad de Fútbol (more commonly Real Sociedad or just *La Real*) from San Sebastián in the Basque Country. It was a Europa League game on a Thursday night towards the end of November. I was sitting near the away end, among a healthy contingent of Spaniards – perhaps 700 or 800, taking the gate to 3,834. They were loud and animated, waving blue and white flags and drumming, chanting and singing throughout. Monaco's small but resolute group of ultras did their best to match them, so that, despite a typically sparse crowd at the Stade Louis II, the likes of former Manchester United player Adnan Januzaj, playing well on the wing for Sociedad, and Monaco's star striker Wissam Ben Yedder (who would go on to be Ligue 1's joint top scorer, with Kylian Mbappé, in 2019/20) had a sense of occasion rather than ennui.

Amid all this, the only English voice I anticipated hearing was John's. We'd come to the game with Doumé and another friend, Luciano, an Italian architect who lives in Menton. As we queued at the turnstiles, Monaco's diligent security men confiscated our main podcast equipment, two Samson Q2U microphones and a Zoom H4n audio recorder, making us leave them in a cabin outside the stadium. This would be the only time we'd fail to get the gear inside a ground. We pressed on, recording with our back-up equipment, two small lavalier mics. They duly ran out of juice just after John had recorded Luciano revealing the secret to making a perfect spaghetti carbonara. Even John's voice, not one that is ever knowingly reticent, was in danger of dilution and yet, with the first half ending 2-1 to Monaco, here was a lot of English being spoken by a bunch of lads from the Midlands. I decided to use my phone to record what I could of the rest of the game and approached the lads to ask what had brought them here.

Dom turned out to be their spokesman. This was their third European match in three nights. They'd started at the Camp Nou with Barcelona v Benfica on Tuesday, 23

November. 'It was very wet but we embraced the rain,' said Dom. 'Adel Taarabt had a blinder.' I'd lost track of Taarabt's career. He was a genius for QPR from 2009 to 2013, especially under Neil Warnock. I'd interviewed Warnock before the Championship-winning 2010/11 season, an experience which confirmed two things: first, in person Warnock is charm itself, a million miles from his raging touchline persona, and secondly, as he put it, 'Adel is wayward, to put it mildly.' I was pleased to learn from Dom and his mates that Taarabt had apparently played so well that the Barça fans gave him a standing ovation.

Next up, Dom and co had flown to Milan for Inter Milan's 2-0 Champions League win against Shakhtar Donetsk. 'The San Siro was amazing, it was the highlight.' Now here they were in Monaco, witnessing Real Sociedad have the better of the possession but not the breaks. *La Real* – 'the real kings of Spain', so-called as a land grab on the notion of Spanish footballing royalty at the expense of Real Madrid and Real Betis – were a fine footballing side, but Monaco put in a performance that was a world apart from the 2-0 home defeat to Marseille. The score remained 2-1; Monaco would top Group B in the Europa League, meaning a guaranteed game in the round of 16 against Sporting de Braga from Portugal.

Dom and his crew would be flying back to Gatwick the following day, on a 7am flight. They popped into my mind a few days later, when I received a text message from Rob Cox, Sonny's father. 'Sonny in squad tonight for FA Cup replay against Bradford,' it said. Before the season began, Brighton had come in for Sonny, but Exeter City had dug their heels in; he'd also had a trial at Manchester

United, where he only just missed the cut. 'They said he'd walk into virtually every other Premier League club,' Rob told me. 'But at United they need to feel 100 per cent that he'll be the next Mason Greenwood – playing in the first team by the time he's 18. One of the coaches was sure, the other three weren't quite.'

Sonny was a sub but didn't come on in what was a 2-1 win for the Grecians. Those English lads at the Stade Louis II knew their football. It was weirdly reassuring to think that, sooner or later, they'd know all about Sonny Cox.

7

December 2021

Living in a Moment of Chaos

'THAT WAS the history of Marseilles, and always had been. A utopia. The only utopia in the world. A place where anyone, of any colour, could get off a boat or a train with his suitcase in his hand and not a cent in his pocket, and melt into the crowd. A city where, as soon as he'd set foot on its soil, this man could say, "This is it. I'm home."'

I'd finished Jean-Claude Izzo's *Total Chaos* just before a trip to the noir novelist's home city on Saturday, 4 December. On the menu: Olympique de Marseille v Stade Brestois 29; *Les Phocéens* v *Les Pirates*. Marseille had only lost twice all season, and a 1-0 win at Nantes the preceding Wednesday meant they'd extended their unbeaten run to six games. But although their Brittany-based opponents hadn't won in Marseille in two decades, they were on fire. Five wins on the bounce included two serious scalps in Monaco and Lens. Still, this was Marseille, second-placed behind Paris Saint-Germain in Ligue 1 and with players of the calibre of Dmitri Payet, emerging Brazilian international Gerson and fit-again Polish striker 'Arek' Milik.

Moreover, Brest might be punching above their weight, but the club from the port town in the Finistère department were used to playing at the Stade Francis-Le Blé in front of an average crowd of some 11,700. Today, they'd be playing in the Stade Vélodrome, France's biggest football ground. Its capacity is 67,394, the average attendance is just under 54,500, and just about every single person present is a fanatical Marseille supporter. I'd seen and heard them take over the Stade Louis II when Marseille comfortably beat Monaco. I'd recently legalled a story for *Huck* magazine by Frank L'Opez, a Londoner living in Marseille, which left no room for doubt: Marseille's ultras were the ultras among ultras. L'Opez had spent time with them, chronicling their help 'for those most in need', donning an Ultras bib to hand out 'cakes and mangoes to migrants and the homeless'. Staunchly left-wing, Marseille's ultras were 'a movement battling against the sanitisation of what they love the most'.

In his story, entitled 'The Ultras of Marseille are fighting for the city's soul', L'Opez quoted one of them, a tough-looking 32-year-old skinhead called Gabo, thus: 'Our role is to put madness in the stadium, to push the team and to create the gigantic banners that you see covering a whole stand that we set fire to afterward. We fill the stadium with our voices and smoke to live in this moment of chaos. If you don't sing we kick you out. If you're a real Ultra, you sweat as much as those on the pitch.'

Marseille's fans weren't just a 12th man. They were as integral to the club as its players. And Marseille itself,

Izzo's Marseille. A claustrophobic headache of colour, sun, sea, racism; streets and bars and food and drink, always *pastis;* guns, gangsters, rape and violence. For Izzo's hero, world-weary, cynical but honest policeman Fabio Montale, Marseille was less utopia, more a city where 'dawn is merely an illusion that the world is beautiful'. But Izzo casts Montale, an outsider of Italian provenance, as embracing those arriving without a cent in their pockets, those who want to call Marseille home – mainly Arab immigrants, who are serially scorned and humiliated by Montale's colleagues in the police.

When an immigrant, an Arab college girl called Leila, is murdered, Montale swears revenge. Izzo's plot echoes the book's title, and his staccato style can be wearing, but as a hymn to the madness of Marseille it is probably unrivalled, and as reading material on the team bus (or plane, given how far Brest had to travel) it was surely to be avoided:

'Marseilles isn't a city for tourists. There's nothing to see. Its beauty can't be photographed. It can only be shared. It's a place where you have to take sides, be passionately for or against. Only then can you see what there is to see. And you realise, too late, that you're in the middle of a tragedy. An ancient tragedy in which the hero is death. In Marseilles, even to lose you have to know how to fight.'

How on earth would Brest cope?

My apprehension on behalf of *Les Pirates* only grew when we entered the Stade Orange Vélodrome. Thanks to Alex Thompson, aka The Navigator – back on land in Sanremo and desperate to see some more football – we'd arrived early enough to soak up the atmosphere. Nav deserves his name. John and I could be late for a game even if we slept in the stadium the night before. There's no nonsense with the Nav. He drove us smoothly to Marseille, in good time for lunch at a restaurant near the Stade Vélodrome called Un Jardin en Ville. It was a fairly upmarket place, packed with quietly conversing Marseille fans. No such reserve once we were inside the Vélodrome. France's longest-serving ultra group, the Commando Ultra 84, were in full voice, led by the *capos,* orchestrators who would spend almost the entirety of the game facing the crowd rather than the pitch. All around the ground, there would be call and response as other ultra groups added to the din. Above us, the sky began to darken, turning a livid pink and navy blue. It, and the noise, could be a harbinger of nothing but ill for Brest.

As usual, we had failed to find anyone selling a programme, and so I didn't know if a player I'd read about, Paul Lasne, was in the starting 11 for *Les Pirates.* Lasne's father Laurent was a writer, journalist and editor. During *confinement* in spring 2020, Lasne Jnr had been moved to follow in his dad's footsteps, writing his own book. It was called *MurMures.* From what I could deduce, it was a book of poetry, celebrating the unexpected disruption to the rhythm of Lasne's life as a professional footballer. Now, at last, he could spend time with his children. To go slow was not to be a shirker.

Lasne's book had received plenty of attention; he struck me as atypical among his peers. I expect he'd have got on well with Dave Sexton, one of football's quietest and yet most eloquent managers, had they been of the same era. Sexton, in an interview with David Williams for

The Independent of 7 March 1993, quoted the American poet Robert Frost on the poet's craft. Frost said, 'The individuality of the words is at least as important as their union.' This statement had a profound effect on Sexton: he felt it applied to coaching too. Sexton died in 2012; another QPR player-manager, Gareth Ainsworth, is known to enjoy poetry. But literary types are few and far between in football. Aside from Lasne, I could think of no other professional footballer who had also published a collection of poetry.

But *MurMures* translates as *Whispers*. The incendiary fervour of *Les Marseillais* grew and grew. Kick-off was upon us. Poor Brest needed more than whispers if they were to emerge from this game without a complete mauling, and Marseille, playing what looked like a 4-3-3 formation (to Brest's 4-5-1, *sans* Lasne), began at a rate of knots. Jorge Sampaoli's men were crisp, quick and accurate, with Gerson drawing a fine early save from Marco Bizot in the Brest goal before a nice one-two with Payet enabled him to surge through the visitors' back line and smash a left-footed shot into the top of the net. Gerson's first few outings with Marseille had been lacklustre; today the €22m signing from Flamengo, who'd had spells in Serie A with Roma and Fiorentina, was on his game. He was sharp and focused. With Payet and David Luiz-lookalike midfielder Matteo Guendouzi also on form, Marseille were an unstoppable blur of white, so much so that Eric, an estate agent from the Var sitting next to me, had no doubt of the final score in view of the 1-0 to Marseille at half-time. 'We are looking very good, really. I think we will win 4-0.'

But *Les Pirates* got lucky. In the 51st minute, a Brest counter-attack led to a handball in the penalty area by Marseille defender Boubacar Kamara. A VAR check confirmed what the referee thought he saw: penalty. Romain Faivre, who would move up to Ligue 1 with a move to Lyon in the January transfer window, converted it. Marseille were rattled. Guendouzi went close after more good work by Payet. But the longer the game went on, the more Brest came into their own. Defensively, they were impenetrable; their swift counter-attacks grew in ferocity until a Brest one-two to rival Marseille's in the first half saw them take the lead. Jérémy Le Douaron was the provider, setting up Franck Honorat with a back-heel. Honorat smashed a right-footed shot in off the underside of the crossbar for 2-1, and there it stayed, Gerson inexplicably spurning the chance for what should have been an equaliser in the final 15 minutes.

Brest had been winless over the past two decades at the Stade Vélodrome, with only one victory at all in their past nine games against Marseille. Now their manager, Michel Der Zakarian, had just taken his side's run to six successive wins, and had done so in one of world football's most intimidating venues. His counterpart, Sampaoli, who'd paced his technical area ever since Kamara's handball, had been well and truly plundered. The few Bretons in the Vélodrome had never seen anything like it. Eric, the estate agent from the Var, looked as if he might be sick.

Afterwards, in a bar near the stadium, Marseille's fans seemed resigned rather than angry. Perhaps they had a sneaking admiration for Stade Brestois 29, whose tactical nous had been perfect. No one expected a Brest result here in the far south, not against France's nine-time Ligue 1 champions, two-time double winners, ten-time Coupe de France victors and, thanks to a 1-0 win over AC Milan in Munich's Olympiastadion in 1993, the only French club to be crowned UEFA Champions League winners. This was the club of Eric Cantona, Laurent Blanc, Didier Deschamps, Didier Drogba, Jairzinho, Rudi Völler, Fabien Barthez and a gallery of other stars, not forgetting Chris Waddle and Tony Cascarino. Even Joey Barton had turned out for Marseille, and while I never much liked him when he was at QPR, Eric, *l'agent immobilier,* had a different view, 'He was a warrior, a true warrior. We loved him.'

All the history counted for nothing on the night. Stade Brestois 29 deserved their win. The ultras did not call the players back on to the pitch, to lambast them, as L'Opez reported when they suffered a 3-2 home defeat to Lens. Mourning the recent death in a car crash of a young ultra from the Fanatics, Clément, emotions were running high. The Vélodrome honoured Clément with a banner in his name, clapping and chanting, '*Olé olé olé Clément Clément, olé olé olé Clé-ment Clé-ment*'. They kept up their fervour, for their team and their lost comrade, until the final whistle.

L'Opez watched as the players headed straight for the tunnel; no stopping to say thanks to the fans. As L'Opez put it: 'The stand erupts in violent insults. One *capo* turns to face the pitch and barks down his megaphone at the team's captain. "Hey Payet, Payet!" he shouts, his arms up in a V. "You go, go get your players … you get them and you bring them here!" He firmly points down to the goal line.

'There is a sudden silence. Quickly, eight of the 11 players who ended the game on the pitch make their way back out. The stadium is almost empty, but in the North and the South, the Ultras stand their ground. "Come here," commands the megaphone. The millionaire footballers make their way over sheepishly. They look frightened, ashamed.

'"We have barely seen you for two years," says the *capo*. "But we are always here. You know that Clément died as he returned from supporting you, as we do, every time. You need us." The whole stand glares at them. "We need you." The players, eyes down, begin to clap with hands above their heads. In the East Stand, an advert board for a bank flashes ominously.'

Driving back to Menton, I tried to make sense of Marseille. I'd seen nothing of the city. I couldn't make any real judgements. But I'd come here, beyond the Italian and French Rivieras, because of Marseille's potent, overwhelming spell. The Marseille of Jean-Claude Izzo, the Marseille of legendary footballers, the Marseille that was the first French team to win a game at Anfield (1-0 in a Champions League fixture in 2007); the Marseille of the wondrous Stade Vélodrome, the Marseille of romance, of tumult, of stately harbourside buildings and deprived inner-city projects; the Marseille of beauty and of chaos. If I were to turn up without a cent, was it a city I could call home? Or was Marseille more likely to result in the fate of James Hanley's Captain Marius, depicted in his novel *The Closed Harbour* as trying to build his life up again after a tragedy at sea (for which he seems to have been at fault), roaming like an automaton among the dockside shipping companies, asking for a position as a captain, being constantly rebuffed, until neither the solace of *pastis* nor a prostitute called Lucy can prevent his descent into insanity.

Hanley wrote, of Marius, 'Against his own will he was falling into the pattern of this storming and thrusting life; he felt like a worn out cog; he fitted nowhere into the machine.'

But as L'Opez quoted Eddy, a 40-year-old member of the Fanatics: 'Don't forget the cannons on the fort walls were not to defend the city, but trained on the people of Marseille itself. It will always be a rebel city.'

Was that why I loved Marseille? I'd been there for about as much time as I'd been in Genoa, all those years ago as a 16-year-old.

And yet, like Genoa – and like Stan Bowles – Marseille enchanted me. It was a city of multitudes, a city of possibility, a city of dreams. And, in the delirium I'd seen at the Stade Vélodrome, unlike anything I'd ever see again at a football match.

A few days later I was back in Genoa for the *Derby della Lanterna:* Genoa v Sampdoria. Did I want some more delirium? On a bitterly cold Friday night, this game delivered in spades.

* * *

The journey to the game was uneventful. On Friday, 10 December, John and I met at lunchtime and boarded a train at Menton-Garavan, to travel the 12 minutes or so to Ventimiglia in Italy. There was enough time in Ventimiglia for a coffee in one of the cluster of cafes near the train station, before getting on the train to Genoa. We were able to work for most of the two-hour trip, our only distraction ourselves, a typically chatty Italian man (as Tim Parks reveals in *Italian Ways*, Italians tend not to appreciate a fellow passenger's desire for solitude, insisting on conversation in the face of the most resolute inscrutability) and the sea.

The Genoa-Ventimiglia line dates back some 150 years, and hugs the Ligurian coast; the sea is constant. Stopping in Varazze, I remembered the road trip with my parents, swimming, Cristina. Where was she now? What was she doing? We'd kept our promise to keep in touch, writing regularly for a year. I no longer know whether she and I cooked up the idea, or our parents, but a plan was concocted that would see Cristina come to stay with me in Devon for three weeks at the beginning of the summer holidays, then I'd go to stay with her in Milan for three weeks. We'd written and written; the expectation, the anticipation, the excitement. I can remember it to this day.

Unfortunately, it all went wrong, almost from the first day we were together. I was immature, a young lad with issues, drawn to booze and recklessness. Cristina wanted no part of a night out with me and my mates. My rampaging nocturnal self was of no appeal, and she wanted no part of daytime discourse either. We stumbled through the three weeks in Devon, occasionally getting on but a long way from enjoying the romance we'd both anticipated. Cristina taught Mum how to cook zucchini the Italian way (fried). My parents have fond memories of Cristina to this day, so too my brother Chris. Despite everything, I do too – she had a habit of calling me 'Mr

Alexander Wade', which I rather liked – and I imagine, and sincerely hope, that Cristina has lived a rich and happy life. But we weren't an item. Nevertheless, and again I can't recall who made the decision, I ended up going to Milan, flying there with Cristina, to be picked up at the airport by her father. We spent a couple of days at the family home in Milan, before leaving for a village called Brumano, 31 miles north-east of Milan in the province of Bergamo.

I'd never forgotten Brumano and the three weeks I spent there. Not because of some new-found maturity and the sudden blossoming of a meaningful relationship between Cristina and me. No, we were cordial, but that was it. She and her family left me to my own devices. And I discovered, on the first day, that in the middle of the village was a football pitch, and on the pitch, each day, all day, there were enough local lads for games of anything from six- to 11-a-side. I joined them. They accepted me. We played football for hours on end. I was fast and skilful; they all had fantastic touches. *Il ragazzo inglese è forte.'* I'd never forgotten one of younger players saying this to a couple of older lads who turned up one day (or something like it – I don't speak Italian and my mind remembers these sounds). They accepted me too. We played and played and played.

Those three weeks in Brumano were the happiest days of my life. And, as the train pulled away from Varazze, suddenly I wondered: was it Brumano, not Genoa, that made me fall in love with the Mediterranean? Had the two places somehow been conflated into a blur of unreliable memories, half-realised fancies that had helped bring me back to live on the Med but whose wellspring was as much mountainous as coastal? The dissonance was welcome; I toyed with it as I checked into my hotel in Genoa's old town, chatting with the receptionist, Irene, about *Il Grifone*, a tattoo of whom was on her left arm. 'We will lose tonight, Sampdoria are better,' said Irene, and something in the way she said this, English words in such a strong and unvarnished Italian accent, made me resolve there and then to return to Brumano before the season was over.

* * *

It was the *Derby della Lanterna*. The biggest game in town, named after the Lanterna di Genova, until 1902 the tallest lighthouse in the world and still the fifth-tallest today. Built of stone in the form of two squares, each capped by a terrace and, on the lower, Genoa's coat of arms – the St George Cross – the Lanterna is on the hill of San Benigno in the city's Sampierdarena district. A lighthouse is believed to have stood on the same site since 1128; a lamp fuelled by olive oil was installed in 1326. Today, a lantern crowns the lighthouse, emitting two white flashes, five seconds apart, every 20 seconds. Antonio Colombo, uncle of Genoa's great explorer Christopher Columbus, was one of the keepers of the lighthouse in 1449.

The *Derby della Lanterna* pits Genoa, Italy's oldest club, against Sampdoria, the new kid on the block. Genoa, formed in 1893, v Sampdoria, created by the merger in 1946 of two clubs, Sampierdarenese and Andrea Doria. In fact, a version of the derby was first contested in 1902, when Genoa played Andrea Doria. Local side Liguria were also known to enjoy spicy confrontations with the illustrious Griffins. But the creation of Sampdoria was accompanied by something guaranteed to up the ante: Sampdoria would share Genoa's ground, the Stadio Luigi Ferraris.

Ever since, Genoa v Sampdoria has been a fixture like no other in Italy. There's a book about it – *The Infinite Derby*, by Renzo Parodi, in which Genoa are cast as superior 'absolutists', capable only of believing in their one club, while Sampdoria's inferiority complex means they are 'relativists', unable ever to forget about the bigger, older brother who grudgingly lets them play on his pitch, happy if Samp win, doubly so if that win is accompanied by a Genoa defeat. For me, the parallel between QPR and Chelsea is obvious. QPR fans do not like Chelsea, for all manner of reasons. No QPR fan can argue that QPR is a more successful club than Chelsea, and yet, during all the years of what is not so much underachievement but of achieving exactly the highs and lows to be predicted of a club of QPR's size (the 'biggest, smallest club' in English football, as local lad turned star striker Kevin Gallen has it), I can testify to feeling a warm glow of pleasure whenever Chelsea lose. On the other hand, as life has gone on and I've met Chelsea fans – even (*la vache!*) becoming friends with one – it is clear that Chelsea fans barely register QPR's existence.

Unless, that is, the two clubs meet. A clash between QPR and Chelsea, whether at Loftus Road or Stamford Bridge, is not a fixture to be taken lightly. The enmity is palpable outside either ground; a heavy police presence is certain. But there is a difference. Samp's ill will to Genoa is said to spring from the club's roots in Italian working-class communities: native dockers against the lofty Englishmen abroad who decided to set up Genoa. The rough and ready against the aristocrats. Not so, QPR v Chelsea. Kings Road might be near Stamford Bridge, but so too are many council estates.

There's also a flavour of irony to the rivalry between Genoa and Sampdoria. Violence has erupted between them, most notably in May 1989 and September 2007, but there's plenty of humour, too. Flags brandished by Griffins tease Sampdoria with *Ospiti di Genova* – 'Guests of [the city of] Genoa'. In 1990, in the midst of Sampdoria's heyday, the derby saw Genoa go into the game without a win against Samp in 13 years. It was 25 November, and it looked like another defeat for *Il Grifone* was on the cards when they went down 1-0 to a Gianluca Vialli penalty. But Genoa fought back, the 'away' team for the day against table-topping Sampdoria, snatching a 2-1 win. The winning goal, a thunderous free kick by Genoa's Brazilian left-back Branco, was recreated on Christmas cards – duly sent to every Samp fan by the joyous *Grifone*.

Better yet was what happened when the *Blucheriati* (another of Sampdoria's nicknames) were relegated to Serie B at the end of the 2010/11 season. Playing at home at the Stadio Luigi Ferraris, Sampdoria slumped to a 2-1 defeat to Palermo. They were down. Their captain, Angelo Palombo – who appeared 459 times for the club and was capped 22 times by Italy – wept on the pitch. Genoa's supporters chose to rub salt in Palombo's and Sampdoria's wounds. Safely mid-table, with nothing to play for in their match on 22 May 2011 against Cesena, they held a five-minute silence to commemorate Sampdoria – and then, having won 3-2, they staged a mock funeral through Genoa's streets. Footage is still available online, posted by Ultras Genoa 1983. It's extraordinary. Some 30,000 people turned up to watch as pallbearers paraded a coffin draped in Sampdoria blue and white through the city, with 'priests' on hand and a 'widow' dressed in black (who seemed to laugh more than she wept). Flares and fireworks completed a carnival attended by almost three times Genoa's average home gate this season.

How would Genoa v Sampdoria, kicking off at 9pm on Friday, 10 December, turn out? John, Nav and I had no idea what to expect. We'd come to love the Stadio Luigi Ferraris, and we knew we'd be sitting near the north end, which is traditionally Genoa's end. Collectively, I'd put our pre-match feelings of excitement at a solid seven out of ten. But on the back of Marseille at home to Brest, this game – any game – would have to go some to hit the same heights.

Nav picked us up in the Piazza Fontane Marose, on the edge of the Old Town. There were no trains back to Ventimiglia later that night, so we'd had to book hotels, while Nav, always unruffled, always capable, had laid his hands on the company car. He was happy to drive to the ground and, yet again, we owed getting smoothly to a game to the young Birmingham City fan we'd met on the train to Genoa v Fiorentina a few months before. And once we'd parked, which took some ingenuity (the whole area was packed), and once we'd walked a few hundred yards to the bars near the stadium, and there, when we began to hear the firecrackers before turning a corner and seeing what resembled a scene out of *Apocalypse Now*, we knew. It was bedlam. Hordes of *Grifone* were marching down a street, chanting and singing with flags aloft, flares lighting up the night sky, police looking on impassively. Adrenaline coursed through freezing December air. Where were Sampdoria's fans? Then I realised: we'd parked to the north-west of the Stadio Luigi Ferraris. This was the home side's turf. All around us was the red and black of Genoa, yellow-gold griffins and St George's Cross flags.

We found a bar on the Via Jean Monnet, which runs along the western side of Stadio Luigi Ferraris. Here, fans from both clubs mingled. Likewise in another bar up a side street, where we ate some indifferent focaccia. The febrile intensity of the procession we'd walked into had gone. The blue shirts of Samp fans mingled peacefully with Genoa's red and black. Jean Monnet, a diplomat and founding father of the European Union, would have been proud. Nevertheless, stopping at a stall outside the ground, so that Nav could buy a hat – it was bitterly cold – a collective decision was made. We would be sitting near the north end, with Genoa fans. The only hat available bore the Sampdoria name. Nav bought it and turned it inside out.

Inside the Stadio Luigi Ferraris, the noise was deafening. Huge flags and banners dominated the north and south ends, punctuated by flares. Music blared through the PA system. Young lads stood on the thin metal railings above the entrance points to the stadium, bouncing up and down, somehow defying physics and not falling 15ft on to the hard concrete below. This was set to be a tough game for Genoa and their recently installed new manager, Andriy Shevchenko. The former Dynamo Kyiv and Chelsea striker had been brought in to replace Davide Ballardini, in a bid to keep Genoa in Serie A. Having taken Ukraine to the quarter-finals of UEFA Euro 2020 (where they lost to England), and with a stunning career as a player behind him, Shevchenko struck Genoa's new owners, United States investment firm 777 Partners, as a certain saviour for *Il Grifone*. But had even he ever experienced anything like this?

Shevchenko had not had a convincing start. His team had picked up just one point in their first four games under his management (although the three defeats were against heavyweights Roma, AC Milan and Juventus), and were 19th in Serie A. A win would see them move out of the relegation zone. Could they do it? On paper, Sampdoria weren't having a hugely better season. Roberto D'Aversa's side had won four, drawn three and lost nine of their 16 league games to amass 15 points, a mere five more than Genoa's tally. But, usually playing in a 4-4-2 formation, they knew how to score, netting 22 times in their 16 matches. And having seen both sides play by now, I agreed with Irene, the receptionist in my hotel. Genoa were lumpen. They were unimaginative. They had no zest. Their best player, Goran Pandev, was 38. Sampdoria were slicker and quicker, a decent footballing side and, unlike Genoa, not beset by injuries (Genoa had seven players sidelined because of injury). And, in Antonio Candreva, Sampdoria had a game-changer.

Amid the mayhem, the game kicked off, and within seven minutes Samp were ahead. Candreva – of course – swept a perfect right-footed cross into the penalty area. It took a slight deflection before being met by the head of the unmarked Manolo Gabbiadini. It was an easy goal for the striker who'd been with Southampton from 2017 to 2019, but not as easy as the chance that fell to Francesco Caputo early in the second half. Again Candreva's contribution was telling. Played in by Gabbiadini, he hit a right-footed shot on the angle that Genoa's keeper, Salvatore Sirigu, stopped then spilled to Caputo's feet. Caputo stabbed the ball into the net with his right boot, then ran to the barrier behind the goal. Jumping on to it, his pure joy transmitted itself to *La Samp*'s cheering fans, all the more so when, with a quick gesture of his right hand, Caputo invited them to have a drink or ten. Pandev had just about Genoa's only moment in a largely scrappy game, turning well on the edge of the six-yard box to shoot narrowly wide in the 64th minute. But then, three minutes later, Caputo and Gabbiadini linked up well for Gabbiadini to strike a low, strong shot with his left foot. It took a deflection and was chalked up as an own goal by Belgian defender Zinho Vanheusden.

That looked to be that, but suddenly Genoa decided to start playing. Mattia Destro, who'd come on early in the second half, was combative and eager, and got a goal back for his team with a header in the 78th minute. *Il Grifone* were giving it a go, but there was Candreva, again, technically excellent and always so intelligent, blasting the ball against the post in the dying minutes. To their credit, Genoa kept trying, Vanheusden also hitting the post, but after 98 minutes the referee called time. Sampdoria were deserved 3-1 winners of this *Derby della Lanterna* and, to look at the way their players celebrated, you'd have thought they'd just won the *Scudetto*. The whole squad and all the club's staff rushed on to the pitch, holding hands, running and knee-sliding on the pitch in front of their devotees in the south stand. They jumped and cheered and punched the air, faces rapt with ecstasy, oblivious of everything and anything save this one small yet huge thing: they had the bragging rights for this most livid of Italian derbies.

Nav felt they overdid it. 'There's no need for the way they're carrying on,' he said. 'It's over the top.' And as we continued to watch the frenzy of jubilation, it struck me that if Sampdoria had won their European Cup Final against Johan Cruyff's Barcelona – if they hadn't been denied by a Ronald Koeman free kick in extra time – their rapture couldn't have been greater than that which we were witnessing. This was a win that went to the core of the club, its players and their very identity.

At the other end, Genoa's fans threw flares on to the pitch. A massive banner was unfurled, hoisted over the heads of the many remaining *Grifone* fans. It said '*Diffidati*' ('Beware'). Boos, whistles and jeers rang out at the men in black and red. They made their way to the north end; there was no scuttling off after a defeat, à la Marseille, to risk being called back by their ultras.

Standing in the penalty box, Genoa's players started to clap their fans. The fans' discontent only intensified. The players stopped applauding. They stood still, faces expressionless, staring into the mass of indistinguishable faces in the north end.

8

January 2022

In the Land of the Lamborghinis (and Elsewhere)

ENGLAND OVER Christmas 2021 was grey, foggy and cold. I went for a few runs for the first time since my knee op. Not very far, just a couple of miles each time, but if I was slow I was also pain-free. Two miles became three, then, one miraculous day, four. For a whimsical moment or two, I wondered if I might even play football again. But no. I was 55. I'd been past it for years. I'd been lucky to play for as long as I had and now needed to move on. I went for a few more runs, back down at the two-to-three-mile distance. I told myself I'd add running to my swimming routine once we were back in France.

We saw our families and friends, had a wonderful Christmas, and I felt conflicted. Was the UK home? Or was Menton home?

It didn't matter. We'd made a decision. We would return to the UK in summer 2022. Ours would be two years in the Alpes-Maritimes, as we'd originally intended.

The curveball of my desire to stay longer in France had been swatted away by the call of family, and, out of the blue, a job offer. I'd spent the past 30 years blending work as a lawyer, writer, editor and journalist; now, in a development no one, least of all me, saw coming, I was offered the CEO role in a specialist media law firm. The company didn't mind if I stayed in France – and a byproduct of the pandemic is, of course, that remote working is now not just accepted but almost the norm – but there was no getting away from the reality: running a UK law firm is easier if you live in England than the south-eastern corner of France.

We made another decision. We'd sell our place in Cornwall and try and buy somewhere in Wiltshire, so, upon our return to the UK, Caroline could be close to her father, brother and extended family. Moreover, returning to live in Penzance didn't chime with the new job. Penzance to London was a six-to-seven-hour drive. The train came in at about the same time. If we were going to live in Penzance, we might as well stay in France.

A lot of change was in the offing. I felt fine about it. It was logical. It all made perfect sense. But then, back in France on 2 January, I had a sensation I hadn't experienced before. Driving along *La Provençale*, dropping down into Menton (*la Perle de la France*), I felt as if I was coming home. The light, the warmth, the lemons, the sea; the school-run routine, L'Amie du Pain, swimming; watching Maud blossom and learn French, walking the dogs high in the mountains above the town: all seemed to welcome me, all pushed a phrase a friend, writer Philippe Anno, had taught me a few years ago, on a holiday in Menton: *je me sens chez moi.* I feel at home.

I put all this to one side. I had a lot of work to do. I had to agree terms for the new role. There was the paperwork and logistics for selling the house in Cornwall. There was Maud, our dogs, all the things that make up a family life. It wouldn't do to dwell on the concept of home; there wasn't time either.

And to my delight, having not seen any football since the *Derby della Lanterna*, there was Nice v Nantes on the evening of Friday, 14 January.

* * *

Delight, but also unease. This was a 9pm kick-off at the Allianz Riviera, where everything had gone so badly wrong on my first visit. Assuming there were no mistakes this time, we'd still be leaving the ground late. It was a near sell-out, too. What time would we get back to Menton?

Our first concern turned out to be whether we'd get to the stadium in time for kick-off. John and I were joined by Luciano, who'd accompanied us to a couple of Monaco games, and an English expat friend, Paddy Kennedy. Luciano knew Nice well and insisted we had time to disembark from the Menton to Nice-Ville train and find somewhere near Nice's Old Town for a pre-match meal. He was probably right, but we happened upon Les Copains in Rue Lascaris – the classic *resto du coin*, the kind seldom seen in Menton. Soon we were tucking into plates of Provençale *daube*, beef braised in red wine, garlic, herbs, spices and vegetables. Perhaps it was again because of lockdown and not really going anywhere for our first year in France, but this was the first time I'd eaten this typical Mediterranean dish. Claudia Roden, possibly the Med's most authoritative cook, writes in *Med: A Cookbook*, 'In the 19th century, every inn in Provence had a pot of *daube* in the ashes of the fireplace, ready for hungry travellers stopping on their way. It was served with potatoes, and in places with Italian settlers with polenta or small macaroni.' Ours came with ravioli. It was delicious.

The restaurant itself was warm and intimate, typically French, a pleasing refuge from the news emanating from the UK that day. The *Daily Telegraph* had reported that two parties were held at Downing Street the night before Prince Philip's funeral, smack in the middle of the UK government's ban on indoor mixing. The *Daily Mirror* carried a story about Downing Street's 'wine-time Fridays', held throughout the pandemic; it even had a photograph of the fridge specially bought to ensure the wine was chilled just so. Elsewhere in the media, it transpired Boris Johnson, Britain's prime minister, had commuted between Number 10 and Chequers between 16 March and 27 March 2020, when his government had banned non-essential travel. Presumably, Johnson would say his trips were essential. Not so his attendance at a drinks party in the Downing Street garden during lockdown on 20 May 2020, yet another story of rank governmental hypocrisy doing the rounds. A Downing Street spokesperson apologised to the Queen (Johnson didn't do so himself, presumably because he hadn't attended the parties on the night before Philip's funeral), but the 'Partygate' scandal seemed not to bother Johnson unduly. Then again, what did? I always felt

Johnson was a snarling, amoral snake dressed up as floppy-haired buffoon. To every accusation that he'd degraded the office of prime minister, he seemed to laugh, and why? Because he had nothing but contempt for anyone so dull as playing by the rules. Rules weren't for Boris.

Inside *Les Copains*, all musings on the moral bankruptcy of the British government were happily forgotten. The *daube* was a revelation, the red wine flowed, it was great to be out and doing something different. A heretical thought entered my mind. Perhaps we could stay here instead of going to the game.

Hayat, our *serveuse*, revived my enthusiasm for the football. She'd been talking to Paddy, and, it seemed, was a Nice fan. I asked her who would win tonight. 'Nice will win tonight because, for me, they're the best. *Et Vive Nice!*' Likewise, a couple of *gendarmes* on the way to the stadium, and a snap poll of fans. Everyone was confident of a Nice win.

Once in our seats in the Garibaldi stand at the Allianz – arriving too late, again, to see Mèfi the eagle – we were confused. The club's website said the game was sold out. I'd had to buy our tickets via a secondary site. And yet the stadium had a mere smattering of supporters. It wasn't even a third of the way to its 36,178 capacity; later, I discovered the official attendance was 5,000. Paddy, a clinical psychologist, was the quickest to work out why there were so few people for this battle of second-placed Nice against ninth-placed Nantes. The author, with Arizona Muse, of a book that was due out a week later called *Turn the Tide on Climate Anxiety: Sustainable Action for Your Mental Health and the Planet*, initially Paddy wondered if some form of collective anxiety was keeping the fans away. But then he realised. 'Covid restrictions,' he said. 'That's what it'll be.' Of course, he was right. Lockdown might have ended, in the UK, France and many other countries, but various Covid restrictions remained in place. Covid tests were *de rigueur* for travel, as we'd found on our Christmas return to the UK. Masks were still mandatory in many places, not least the trains in France. And the authorities had clearly decided that, while football could resume with crowds in France, there needed to be plenty of space between supporters.

The sight of Justin Kluivert on Nice's left wing took Paddy and I down a different psychological alleyway – and not because he'd lined up on the right side of the pitch. To be sure, the young Dutchman has some big boots to fill: the 22-year-old's father, of whom he is the spit, is Patrick, of Ajax, Barcelona, Newcastle and the Netherlands national team fame. Capped 70 times by the Netherlands between 1994 and 2004, during which time he scored 40 goals, Kluivert also scored the only and winning goal for Ajax in the 1995 UEFA Champions League Final against AC Milan. He was just 18 at the time. Paddy said he'd seen an interview with Kluivert Sr in which he'd been asked about his son, apparently replying, 'I watch some games, but I don't watch them all. If he's happy, I'm happy.' That sounded a little lukewarm (and later, I found plenty of more conventionally proud fatherly comments online), but Justin, on loan for the season from Roma, was having a good game and was popular with the home crowd. Could he one day equal or even eclipse his father's achievements? It's a tall order that few among the offspring of professional footballers can claim to have met. Paddy put Manchester City's Erling Haaland, son of Alfie of Nottingham Forest, Leeds United and Manchester City, as the most likely. Timothy Weah, son of George, popped into my mind, but while both had scored for Paris Saint-Germain, the son had his work cut out: George is now the president of Liberia.

Nice were on top. They went ahead with a Kasper Dolberg penalty, to quite the acclaim from such a small crowd. Thanks to a found programme, I learnt the game was dedicated to Antoine Bonifaci, who'd played for Nice in the club's 1950s heyday. A midfielder *à la palette sublime*, Bonifaci was capped 12 times by France, each cap coming while he was a Nice player. He'd been a key member of Nice's *Championnat*-winning team in 1951, and won the league and cup double with Nice in 1952. He then hopped east over the border to Italy, where he played for Inter Milan, Bologna, Torino and Vicenza before ending his career with Stade Français in the Vaucresson suburb of Paris. Settling on the Côte d'Azur for the rest of his life, Bonifaci was honoured by the naming of Villefranche-sur-Mer's stadium in his name. A stone's throw from the sea, with views of yachts, villas and low-lying pine trees across the water on Cap Ferrat, the Stade Antoine Bonifaci rivals Cap Ferrat's Stade Intercommunal for the title of Best Appointed Football Pitch in the World. Bonifaci died on 29 December 2021 in Villefranche-sur-Mer. Nice's programme honoured him with a piece entitled *'En Mémoire De L'Immense Antoine Bonifaci'*.

But if *Les Niçois* felt the more enthused because of Bonifaci's memory, their team conceded on the stroke of half-time. Nantes were a decent side, as befits a club which has won Ligue 1 eight times and the Coupe de France three times. I'd read about Nantes's style of play: *jeu à la nantaise*, a collective spirit instilled by various coaches over the years. Playing all in yellow, *Les Canaris* had produced top-quality players, including Marcel Desailly, Didier Deschamps, Claude Makélélé and Christian Karembeu. Under the management of 58-year-old former defender Antoine Kombouaré, could they snatch a win in the second half?

I hoped so, despite the admiration I was developing for Bonifaci, who, the programme revealed, had also won the Italian league title with Inter Milan in 1954. He'd lived until he was 90 and there was no doubting the esteem in which he was held. The eulogy in the programme was as sincere as it was lyrical. Bonifaci had been a local lad, whose parents owned a restaurant, who was blessed with natural talent. '*Bien, très bien*,' said the programme, and then:

'*Tellement bien qu'il devient un immense monsieur alors qu'il n'est pas encore un homme, grâce a ce jeu dont il tire déjà toutes les ficelles.*'

That was some praise. Bonifaci was a star for *Les Aiglons* when he was just 18: a towering figure when he wasn't yet a man, thanks to what he could do with a football. How could anyone not warm to this *immense monsieur*? How churlish would it be not to want Nice to win the game they'd dedicated to him?

There was no logical reason for secretly backing Nantes. Irrationality prevailed, as usual. I recognised the Nantes number two, Fábio Pereira da Silva – better known just as Fabio. He hadn't fared as well as his brother Rafael when the pair signed for Manchester United in 2007, but I felt he put in a shift during his 21 appearances on loan at QPR in our disastrous 2012/13 season (it ended in a paltry four wins and richly merited relegation to the Championship). It was oddly comforting to see Fabio below us on the pitch, but while Luciano, Paddy and I were engaged with the game, John was not. He'd spent the first half struggling with technical issues, and, by the half-time break, had made no progress. His mental state seemed to be edging to mine, last time we were at the Allianz Riviera.

'Do you think you'll be able to solve whatever it us?' I asked, resorting again to my phone to record some material for the podcast.

John was confident. 'Of course.'

Around us, people were curious. This often happened when we'd start recording a podcast. To be fair, two men talking into large microphones in the middle of a crowd is not an everyday event at a football match. But this time round, it was John's sheer absorption in his phone, lavalier mics and cables that prompted their curiosity. Head down, not taking in anything of the game, John was getting more and more frustrated. 'We've got everything set up, it's all powered up, everything should be perfect,' he said. 'But it's not working. It's absent. Like the 36,000 people that are missing – so is our equipment.'

Maybe in the second half – would it come right then?

'It's a possibility,' said John. 'Like the British government, I can't confirm or deny that this is something I attended with a view to being a podcast. I thought this was a work event. I didn't realise I was under any obligation to bring my own drink, I didn't know I had to finish within a certain, prescribed time.'

That seemed to be clear. But it wasn't. Could we, I repeated, solve the equipment issues or not?

'Lessons will be learned and we will grow. I, for one, am shocked and saddened by the developments about the equipment failure. I wasn't aware of the equipment failure. Had I known I would have stated quite clearly that the equipment needs to be remedied, but not knowing that the equipment failed I can only say that I was there in a human capacity and not in an equipment-repairing capacity.'

I asked one further question. 'Is it your position that you did or did not invite the equipment along tonight?'

'Someone from my office invited the equipment along. Now, am I meant to know where the equipment is invited to for every event the equipment should go to? There are events everywhere. There are events turning up, wherever I am or not, and I get invited along, and I turn up for the event, and I'm invited, and then they say it's an equipment event, and I'm like, I didn't know that, I thought it was an event, here's my bottle of cider.'

Nice went on to win 2-1, the clinching goal scored by Khéphren Thuram, son of Lilian. The young defensive midfielder had a good game, but he too had a lot to live up to: Lilian is France's most-capped player, with 142 appearances between 1994 and 2008, a World Cup in 1998 and the UEFA Euro 2000 title too. A fine career with Monaco, Parma, Juventus and Barcelona now sees him active in politics, especially in combatting racism: Thuram is the author of *La Pensée Blanche*, or, in English,

White Thinking: How Racial Bias Is Constructed and How to Move Beyond It. He is also well-known for his activism in support of same-sex marriage.

What a difference from Boris Johnson, the charlatan John riffed on in his equipment failure speech.

Turned out we were missing a vital cable for the match. To my embarrassment, it further turned out it was me who'd left it behind. Paddy found an Uber after the game and we were back in Menton gone midnight. The score was Allianz Riviera 2 John and Alex 0.

But of course it was. For it was here that the England national team went down 2-1 to Iceland on Monday, 27 June 2016 in Euro 2016. Alan Shearer called it the worst performance he'd ever seen by an England team. It was as humbling as the infamous 1-0 defeat to the United States in the 1950 World Cup. And it was England's second exit from Europe in four days: on 23 June, Vote Leave had won the Brexit referendum.

* * *

If the Allianz Riviera was cursed, a far easier game was on offer the following weekend. Rapid Omnisports de Menton were hosting Cagnes-Le Cros on Sunday, 23 January at 3pm. The distance from our house in the Garavan area to Menton's ground, the Stade Lucien Rhein, was half a mile. The distance to Cagnes-sur-Mer, a Riviera town of 52,000 people sandwiched between Nice and Antibes, was just under 30 miles.

This, then, was a local derby, and it didn't look good for the home side. Their manager, Stéphane Collet, told Riviera newspaper *Nice-Matin* that he was 'résignée mais *pas abattu*' after a 3-0 defeat away to Toulon the previous Sunday. Resigned but not defeated, although Collet, who'd had a good career with clubs such as Nice, Strasbourg, Lens and Real Sociedad, might inwardly have been feeling a little less sanguine. He'd had to play three players from his second team against Toulon and was particularly irked by his side's defending. He'd lost a player, Mazzella, to a red card (an '*expulsion*', as the French have it) in the 38th minute. Yet worse, the Toulon defeat was Menton's fifth in a row. They were second from bottom in Regional 1 (Méditerranée), effectively the sixth tier of French football.

In contrast, Cagnes-Le Cros were having a much better season, lying second in the table and with a 1-0 win over Fos-sur-Mer the previous weekend.

It was a balmy day, shorts and T-shirt weather. Flicking through the sports pages of *Nice-Matin* at L'Amie du Pain in the morning, I saw a photograph of a footballer called Paul Wade. He wasn't English; it fact he was a 21-year-old Frenchman born in Cagnes-sur-Mer, who'd scored for Nice II the day before in a National 3 game. I liked the depth and detail of *Nice-Matin*'s football coverage, and I liked its tagline: '*Réseau Social Depuis 1945*' ('Social Media since 1945'). I'd have to look out for Paul Wade, maybe try and catch a Nice II game, but I wasn't sure where the paper was going with its front-page headline that day. '*À Quoi Sert L'Europe?*' rang out in bold black type, below EU imagery, with one subhead asking, '*Pourquoi est-ce important dans notre quotidien?*' What is Europe for? Why is it important in our daily lives?

Not the French too, I wondered, as Maud and I paid the bill, rounded up the dogs and made our way home from L'Amie. Brexit was bad enough. Shouldn't France claim pole position in Europe now, not start doubting whether there's any point in the European Union?

The Mediterranean is visible from the Stade Lucien Rhein – so close that a well-hit volley out of the ground might bobble into the Port du Garavan – and that Sunday afternoon it seemed as if every known watercraft was being piloted on the calm sea. I enjoyed the sight of so many people getting their oceanic fixes. There was Italy, too, to my left, with the mountains sweeping down into the sea. Not a cloud in the sky. I felt so lucky to live in this little pocket of France and now it was time to relax in a crowd of some 60 to 70 and enjoy a pleasant game of football. Caroline and I had even brought Maud along. She'd absorbed the notion of football by dint of my going to so many games, though she insisted I spent my time at a football 'patch' rather than a football 'match'. She clamoured to come along one day. A gentle stroll to Menton's football patch made for her perfect debut game, and a few friends agreed. John and Helén brought their kids, so too Eric and Lydie and Luciano and Holly. Even Menton's kit, light-blue vertical stripes against white, blue shorts and white socks, seemed deliberately chosen to suit the ambiance of the day.

Neither side's players got the same memo. Within minutes, tackles ranging from robust to ruthless were flying in. If there'd been a proper crowd, there would have been roars of outrage. It was difficult to say which team was the worse, but the physios were on and off the pitch to treat stricken players more than at any other game I'd seen along the Mediterranean coastline. Menton were up for it, desperate to end their terrible run – but so were *Les Cagnois*, tearing about the pitch manically rather than, in keeping with the nickname for their hometown of Cagnes-sur-Mer, as if they were genteel citizens of 'the Montmartre of the French Riviera'. Soon enough, there was a sending-off when the Cagnes-Le Cros goalkeeper scythed down a Menton player outside the penalty box. Still the hard tackles continued. My allegiance was to Menton, but Cagnes-Le Cros were well drilled, especially in midfield, and Menton couldn't make anything of their man advantage. Bizarrely, one of their players decided to handle the ball into the Cagnes net when to head it in would have been as easy; goal disallowed. Cagnes started to dominate, hit a post and then, three minutes before half time, went ahead.

Poor Menton. They seemed destined to succumb to a sixth successive defeat. If only they had one of their former luminaries on the pitch, a player like Cédric Varrault, who made 208 appearances for Nice, or even the less acclaimed but solid Frédéric Advice-Desruisseaux, on Lille's books between 2001 and 2004 (and possibly still remembered by fans of Kidderminster Harriers, for whom he played nine times in 2004). If only the great Michel Hidalgo was still alive and could pop in for a half-time talk. Hidalgo was a two-time title-winner with Monaco and one of the French national side's finest managers, taking France to the semi-finals of the 1982 FIFA World Cup and going on to win UEFA Euro 1984 on home soil. Then, Hidalgo orchestrated the *carre magique* (magic square) of four of France's most gifted players, a nigh-on invincible midfield of Michel Platini, Jean Tigana,

Alain Giresse and Luis Fernandez. Before, in 1968/69, he'd been Menton's player-manager. But Hidalgo, who'd settled in the south of France and managed Marseille from 1986 to 1991, died in March 2020, four days after his 87th birthday.

Could Menton at least harness his spirit, his belief that the best football came when players were enjoying the game? The second half began and it didn't look likely. Cagnes-Le Cros seemed even better organised. The wicked challenges and sneaky fouls continued. At this rate, both sides would lose three or four through injury for their next games. And then they did it. Menton finally unlocked the Cagnes-Le Cros defence, scoring five minutes from time.

By then, the mums and children had all long since departed for the nearby Parc du Pian. This football patch had failed to engage them; they could hurtle about freely in the parc, and if you're between three and eight that's more fun than watching the footy. I wondered if Maud, who'd worn a QPR top for the outing, would remember the afternoon. She loved kicking a football and was always talking about football patches. One day I'd take her to QPR and tell her about Chloe Kelly, a lifelong QPR fan and England striker. But this hadn't been a classic and Maud was still only four. As possibly the least well-attended game I'd ever been to (save for those in which I'd played), I doubted she'd retain any sense of it as an occasion.

The referee's whistle sounded. Many players collapsed to the floor, battered and exhausted. A 1-1 draw was just about fair.

Leaving the Stade Lucien Rhein, idly wondering about Maud and football and sure that this had been the most violent game I'd yet seen on the Med, I heard an English voice behind me. I turned round and asked its well-dressed owner, who I'd heard mention Spurs, if he lived here.

'No, we came up from Cagnes-sur-Mer to see our son play,' said the man, his wife at his side.

'Your son? Which one was he?'

Michael Alexander explained that his son Sam, a 19-year-old striker born and bred in Cagnes-sur-Mer, had been wearing the number nine shirt for Cagnes-Le Cros.

'Really?' I said. John and I had noticed Sam, a good ball player who'd hit the post and been a threat throughout. 'He had a good game.'

Michael was understandably proud, 'Yes, he did well today.' We talked some more. Michael and his wife Christine had been living in France for 24 years, since they got together. Sam had been on Nice's books but left at the beginning of the season for Cagnes-Le Cros, to be sure of playing first-team football.

Back in England, Sonny Cox had just done something similar. He'd made his first-team debut for Exeter City on 5 October 2021, coming on as a 49th-minute substitute in a 2-2 draw at Cheltenham Town in the EFL Trophy. Two days before Menton v Cagnes-Le Cros, he'd joined Southern League Premier Division South club Weston-super-Mare for the rest of the 2021/22 season.

Sonny was born on 11 October 2004, Sam on 1 October 2002. A lifetime was ahead of each. Would they make it? Would they fulfil their dreams – and the dreams of their fathers, their mothers, their families?

As I walked the short distance home, the oddest thought arrived. What had the parents of Stan Bowles dreamt of for him?

* * *

Stan was back in my thoughts a few days later. I had to travel to London for work, and the trip coincided with QPR at home to Swansea on 25 January. I'd already read Stan's wonderfully irreverent autobiography, *Stan the Man*, but found myself dipping into it again on the plane from Nice to Heathrow. Perhaps I was juggling two competing notions of identity; certainly, so in thrall to life on the Med as I was, I wondered if I'd have that familiar feeling of coming home on a cold Tuesday night, as I walked through the Loftus Road turnstiles.

I turned to Stan's account of QPR's UEFA Cup quarter-final away game against AEK Athens in 1977. This was as far as QPR ever got in European competition. In his book, did Stan reveal a love of the Med? Did Athens and its nearby glittering sea captivate him? His visit starts well enough: he recalls being given a bouquet of flowers at the airport. The press, though, dubbed it 'a bouquet of barbed wire' – Stan had been threatened with violence by Greeks in London, and UEFA had ordered a special advisor to attend the game. Not for the last time, AEK's future in a European competition was in danger. Stan is as sanguine as ever, accepting the flowers gracefully but then finding that none of the QPR contingent would be allowed to leave their hotel complex. This he counts as one of his regrets:

'I've been to all of these countries – despite a fear of flying – and often been unable to venture outside. But that was the

business we were in, and we had to accept it. At least we had a private beach where we could relax, and join in watersport activities if we felt so inclined, which, of course, I didn't. The Superstars fiasco was still fresh in my mind!'

I stopped reading. One thing seemed clear: Stan didn't love the Med as much as I did, a reason being that he had barely had a chance to experience it. And maybe he wasn't that bothered anyway. But the reference to the 'Superstars fiasco' brought back my childhood memory, aged ten, of *Superstars*. I haven't checked, but I am sure it aired during the long, hot summer of 1976. Anyone of my age and above remembers that summer. Not a drop of rain for weeks. England, especially the south-west where I lived, might as well have been the Med. My friends and I swam and played football every day for the whole summer holiday. Somewhere along the line, I got wind of Stan's appearance on *Superstars*.

I was excited beyond belief. Stan – my hero, the God among sportsmen of the era – was going to be competing. *Superstars* was wildly popular at the time, watched by an average of fourteen million people in the UK alone, and millions more worldwide. Over the show's format, which pitted well-known athletes against each other in sports other than their own, Stan would prevail. Everyone would watch and gasp and comprehend what I and all QPR fans knew – Stan was the best. Why, he only needed to turn up.

In his book, Stan sounds a cautionary note, writing:

'If you made a fool of yourself on this show you did so in front of an awful lot of people.'

Stan, make a fool of himself? Of course not. My idol would win. His fellow competitors, who included

Formula 1 racing driver James Hunt, boxer John Conteh, rugby union legends Gareth Edwards and J.P.R. Williams, track and field athlete David Hemery, Jonah 'Mr Squash' Barrington and judo champion Brian Jacks, would shrink, fade and wither away to nothingness in the face of Bowles's brilliance. For Bowles was brilliant. There could be no doubt about this. I even persuaded my football-indifferent family to stand by for the inevitable triumph of QPR's resident genius.

Mum and Dad may have been blind to football's allure, and they weren't too keen on sport generally, but *Superstars* was an entry-level programme with a straightforward premise. Elite athletes would compete against each other in a variety of sports, eschewing their own sport. They'd be awarded points according to their position in each event. The winner was the competitor with the most points. *Superstars* was simple, easy to follow and great TV.

But Stan wasn't great. He was very far from great. He was the antithesis of great.

Alarm bells sounded in his first event, a swimming race. Stan did not complete a length. Encouragement turned to mute incomprehension. What was he doing? Why wasn't he swimming? Come on, Stan! But after just a yard or two, Stan stopped and clung to the edge of the pool. In his book, the explanation for his stasis is revealed, 'The first event was the swimming and I can't even swim!' Next Stan was in a weightlifting event, but could he lift the weights? He could not. Then came canoeing. Stan was profoundly unhappy in his canoe. Soon he was engulfed by a 3ft wave. The current pushed him into the canoe of fellow competitor and foe, Malcolm

'Supermac' Macdonald. The pair capsized and had to be rescued.

Even the infinite credulity of a ten-year-old could not now conceive of Stan recovering and going on to win *Superstars*. Silence slunk into the sitting room. There we were, clustered round the TV, Mum and Dad showing an interest in their eldest's strange fascination for football, brother Chris watching too, much younger sister Suki possibly also present. We were there for Stan, spectators to behold his superiority. But Stan was useless.

Incredibly, his performance became even worse. In a game of tennis against J.P.R. Williams, he was thrashed 6-0, 6-0. Fair enough, really: many years later I discovered that Williams was a British junior tennis champion. But at the time all I could see was humiliation upon humiliation for my hero. He underperformed in the 100m sprint, which was won by Macdonald. Stan's nemesis, who had just completed a summer transfer from Newcastle to Arsenal, nailed it in 11 seconds, and while Stan's 12.6 seconds was respectable it still left him in fourth place, behind Macdonald, rugby union player David Duckham and another judoka, David Starbrook. Then came the nadir: the shooting. Firing a pistol at a bullseye seemed straightforward enough. Stan contrived to miss with each shot and narrowly missed shooting himself in the foot when, unaccountably, he pulled the trigger and fired a bullet into the table in front of him. The footage is available online. Stan examines the damage the bullet has caused, as if, of course, he'd meant to shoot the table, why wouldn't he? Isn't that what everyone does? To test the bullets? Check the strength of the table? Behind him the other competitors laugh, tittering at first and then openly. James Hunt especially seemed to embrace the moment, though Stan's book refers to 'nervous laughter' rather than hilarity. The reality, for Stan, was that the shooting contest 'was like a scene in a horror film'. This is perhaps hyperbole, but then again, for all that Stan seems unperturbed – for all that Hunt smiles, and commentator David Vine deadpans his way through the incident – who can say what was really going on inside his mind? For that was one of the things about Bowles. Amid all the tabloid tales, the nights out with George Best, the larks with Don Shanks, the battles with the uncompromising defenders of the era, the goals, the glory, the winning horses and the losing bets, there was always an outward impassivity. What did it disguise?

There was one more event, the steeplechase. Memory is dangerous thing; it plays tricks; often the sensibility of past event is all that is certain. My mind's eye has a vision of Stan looking slight, bedraggled and disgruntled in the steeplechase, like a man who's made a mistake but knows he's got to suffer its consequences for a little longer before he's free again. His book suggests this memory is fairly accurate. Stan started well before quickly fading, though there was one triumph: he beat Malcolm Macdonald into last place.

Stan Bowles, on *Superstars*, was a disaster. I scuttled off to my room, feeling like an idiot.

On the plane from Nice to Heathrow, all this came back to me but with Bowles' autobiography I could also refresh my memory some more. To say that Stan did not take *Superstars* seriously would be a grave understatement.

With teammate and general partner-in-mischief Don Shanks acting as his 'manager', the pair seem to have viewed *Superstars* mainly a means to easy readies from the BBC. To this day, Bowles' points tally – seven out of a possible 80 – is the lowest of any *Superstars* competitor. But Stan's book reveals more than merely a laissez-faire attitude to the competition. The night before, Stan and Shanks had been drinking into the early hours with James Hunt – 'he was a nice guy and we had a laugh together' – and turned up for the day's events 'at what seemed like five in the morning … with hangovers the size of Wembley Stadium.' Stan's appraisal of the night before is beautifully blunt, and puts him just as neatly at odds with the finely-tuned athletes against whom he's due to compete. While the other 'heroes' – Stan's book has the word in quotation marks, as if to question what constitutes a 'hero' – are all anxious about the forthcoming contest, skulking seriously around, drinking mineral water and nibbling on cucumber sandwiches, before heading to their beds for an early night, he and Shanks pile into wine, lager and cigars. Somewhere in the depths of the morning, they too depart for their beauty sleep – but by now they can barely stand.

No wonder Stan had performed so badly. No wonder the shooting 'proved to be a 24-carat gold nightmare'. And no surprise that Don Shanks was rebuffed when he told the BBC handler he would train Stan 'to perfection' for next year's Superstars. She shook her head in horror, before saying: 'Next year? Next bloody year? There won't be a next year for you two … goodbye, gentlemen!'

Aged 10, Stan on *Superstars* was an embarrassment. In my adult years, Stan on *Superstars* was a virtuoso. His sheer insouciance, his lack of fear, the strength of character not to care about failing in sports that were not his; his indifference to everything being played out on national television, his honesty, his all-too-flawed battles with the likes of Macdonald: all this was as magnificent as his skill with a football. Reading the autobiography when it was first published in 2004 confirmed this. Likewise, dipping back into it on the plane from Nice to Heathrow. It's got to be one of the best football books ever written.

So yes, when I stepped through one of the South Africa Road turnstiles for QPR v Swansea on Tuesday, 25 January, I had that feeling again. It was great to be back. I was home.

The game ended 0-0, but, as 0-0 draws go, it was a good one. Swansea are a good footballing side, and two of our group of five definitely admired them more than QPR: Tom Watt and Gareth Graham. Tom is an actor turned football writer; I always liked him when he was in *EastEnders*, where he played Lofty Holloway, the barman at the Queen Vic. Our paths had crossed once through a mutual friend, literary agent and QPR fan Jonathan Harris, and more recently via work. Having written many acclaimed books on football, Tom ghost-wrote *Position of Trust: A Football Dream Betrayed*, with Andy Woodward. Detailing the horrific abuse Woodward suffered at the hands of Barry Bennell, when Woodward was a child and Bennell a coach at Crewe Alexandra – and also Woodward's courage in revealing what had happened – *Position of Trust* was published in 2019. It's an important book and I'd been privileged to have the job of the job of legalling it.

Gareth, meanwhile, is a former professional footballer who now works as an insurance broker. A midfielder, Gareth began his career at Crystal Palace, where he made one appearance, and went on to play for Brentford and a dizzying array of clubs in non-league football. We'd worked together for mutual clients in film and publishing and, oddly enough, I'd just seen Gareth's name pop up in another manuscript that had come my way for libel advice – *All Together Now* by Erik Samuelson, former chief executive of AFC Wimbledon and hugely influential in helping Wimbledon return to their Plough Lane roots.

Tom and Gareth are fabulously knowledgeable about football and appreciated Swansea's style – concise, quick and neat passing football, at all times. Another of our party, New York lawyer Cameron Stracher, had never been to a football (or 'soccer', as he would have it) game in the UK before and was suitably neutral. For myself and an old friend, Richard Ager, we only had eyes for the Hoops. We used to go to games at Loftus Road some 25 years ago; I'd also met Richard for the away game at Oxford United, when my son Harry lost his Matchbox car. We hadn't seen each other for a while and Richard was interested in my new life in the south of France.

'Do you think you'll stay there?' he asked.

I told him no, we'd be coming back at the end of the summer. The plan was to sell our house in Cornwall and move closer to Caroline's dad in Wiltshire.

'Only an hour or so on the train to London,' said Richard.

'You're right,' I said. 'I'll get a season ticket and come to Rangers with you.'

* * *

I couldn't believe what I was seeing. Elyes Ayéche, the number ten for Villefranche Saint-Jean Beaulieu, had the quickest feet I'd seen since Adel Taarabt's heyday at Loftus Road. Watching him on a sunny afternoon at the Stade Intercommunal du Cap Ferrat at 2 Boulevard du Général de Gaulle, Saint-Jean-Cap-Ferrat – surely one of the world's best-appointed football grounds – I was blown away. So was John. Ayéche was having a blinder, beating opposing players for fun, pulling off every imaginable trick, back-heeling perfect passes and tormenting FC Rousset Ste Victoire in this Saturday afternoon National 3, Corse-Méditerranée division clash. Villefranche SJB were second from bottom in the table, but you wouldn't have known it to watch Ayéche. He was unplayable. What on earth was he doing, turning out in the lower levels of French professional football? Was he on loan from a nearby giant, maybe Nice or Marseille, finding his form again after a serious injury? He wasn't that young – we reckoned he was in his mid-to-late 20s. Had he once been with a Ligue 1 outfit, only for his career to founder? Or, just maybe, it wasn't too late and a big club was about to make a bid.

We had a perfect view of the Ayéche enigma. Villefranche SJB play on an artificial pitch with Subbuteo-sized terracing on the eastern side. We'd found a spot there, adjacent to, but not amid, a rowdy collection of young fans. 'Mini-ultras', I felt, given not just their youth but also their dedicated emulation of the *capos* we'd seen at Marseille, one of them standing on a chair with a loudspeaker, facing his friends, yelling chants and songs throughout, intensity rising if the response he wanted wasn't loud enough. There were only about 25 to 30 of them, but they made a colossal racket. At times, it was a distracting racket, not least towards the end of the game, when it was clear FC Rousset would be coming away with the points. One of the lads, who was 11 if he was a day, picked up a chair and threw it at the fence between fans and pitch. Then, he started kicking the fence. No one, not even his friends, seemed to notice, but they were doing their best impression of the angry and betrayed, cursing into the heady air of Cap Ferrat. But for most of this game Ayéche was so good we couldn't take our eyes off him. The mini-ultras were interesting, but they weren't compulsive viewing. Ayéche was a must-see, must-watch player, strong, muscular, clever, alert, on his game and, surely, we felt, out on the town that night – if Cap Ferrat is that kind of place – to celebrate steering his side to a much-needed victory.

Only it didn't turn out like that. Just 4,655 people live in Rousset, a village some ten or 11 miles from Aix-en-Provence and 45 miles from Marseille. Here, in the land of Lamborghinis, the footballing lads of Rousset had other ideas. They turned up in Cap Ferrat on Saturday, 29 January, stared down Elyes Ayéche and came away with a precious 1-0 win thanks to a 29th-minute goal against the run of play by their own number ten, Sofiane Sidi Ali. Ayéche kept at it. He was at the heart of every move Villefranche SJB put together and yet somehow Rousset kept him at bay. By the end of the game, Ayéche seemed to tire and, frustration getting the better of him, he picked up a yellow card before being substituted in the final minutes. Rousset, with just four wins so far, nicked a significant 1-0 win.

John and I felt sorry for Villefranche SJB, basically because we'd enjoyed watching Ayéche so much. But as we left, we also felt discombobulated. This had been a good game of football, but it wasn't football as we knew it, not because of the artificial pitch, or the fact that entry was free, or because of the antics of the mini-ultras. It was the setting. A ball kicked out of the ground at the Stade Intercommunal du Cap Ferrat had a good chance of landing on a Ferrari or Lamborghini, or of splashing into the pool of a villa worth millions. The Italianate and belle époque houses here are unaffordable for anyone other than the international super-rich. I'd read that Andrew Lloyd Webber is a resident; nearby, in Villefrance-sur-Mer, Tina Turner apparently has a place. Winston Churchill, Elizabeth Taylor, Richard Burton, David Niven, Charlie Chaplin, Hubert de Givenchy and Baroness Charlotte Béatrice de Rothschild were just some of Cap Ferrat's former denizens. Who can blame them, who could blame anyone, for wanting to live here? Even the German philosopher Friedrich Nietzsche, not a person known for seeing the sunny side, loved the area. There's a path named after him nearby, the *chemin de Nietzsche*, because he adored the Riviera's 'richness of light' and the miraculous tonic effect it had 'on a tortured, sometimes suicidal soul' like his.

It's easy to empathise with Nietzsche. The Cap Ferrat peninsula (a *presqu'île*, almost an island) lies between the bays of Villefranche and Beaulieu and seems to soak up the sun like a magnet. The high, white cliffs above the beach resort of Eze Bord de Mer protect what was once a humble fishing village from northerly winds; there are beaches galore and lush vegetation and, everywhere, the feel of old money. That money might now be spent on the latest Lamborghini, but the sense that it's been in the family since the dawn of time is palpable. Where did the footballers for Villefranche SJB come from? Were they the offspring of millionaires? After the game, did a chauffeur arrive to take them home to a Cap Ferrat mansion in what, in 2012, was named the second most expensive residential location in the world, after Monaco?

Forbes upped Cap Ferrat to first place in 2016, when Villa Les Cédres came on the market. For US $1.1 billion, you could snap up a ten-bedroom villa with a handy ballroom, a 50-metre swimming pool, stables for 30 horses and, for those moments of spiritual rather than worldly need, a chapel. Oh, and a botanical park. Forbes says it's 'considered one of the most beautiful private gardens in Europe. It covers more than 35 acres with 20 greenhouses, is overseen by 15 full-time gardeners, and features some 15,000 rare tropical species, also reportedly Europe's largest collection of tropical plants.' Forbes also quoted le-gotha.com to explain how Saint-Jean-Cap-Ferrat has the most expensive price per square metre – more than €200,000 at the top end – in the world, 'More than 50 of the most beautiful villas of the 600 on the *presqu'île* are worth their weight in gold. It's true that there's very little for sale because the biggest owners in Saint-Jean-Cap-Ferrat are very attached to their sumptuous dwellings, even if they come only some weeks of the year.'

Perhaps Villefranche SJB's footballers weren't locals. Maybe they came from the *banlieues* of Nice; maybe the closest they'd got to owning a Lamborghini was when they smashed a clearance on to its *trop cher* roof.

John and I were tempted by the thought of a drink in one of the restaurants in the old fishing village. Then again, a small beer would probably set us back €30 each.

We hit the road, and, as we drove up a hill near the Stade Intercommunal du Cap Ferrat, we saw the mini-ultras. They were lined up on either side of the road, shouting and cheering and waving flags like bullfighters at approaching cars, only to step aside at the last moment. What next, when they'd got bored, for them? Home to their mums and dads in a house worth more than John and I had earned in our lifetimes, put together? Or the bus to Villefranche-sur-Mer or Beaulieu-sur-Mer, and then the train to Nice-Ville and then out into the suburbs and an altogether different life?

We slowed down, smiled and waved back at them. Wherever they came from, we had a couple of things in common. We all loved football, and we'd all been treated to a cracking performance by Elyes Ayéche.

9

February 2022

La força d'un sentiment

AS CANNES v Villefranche Saint-Jean Beaulieu, Saturday, 5 February 2022. I couldn't wait to see Ayéche play again and was curious about AS Cannes, formed in 1902 and, in 1932, one of the founding clubs of the French First Division. *Les Dragons* came second in the league that year and, also in 1932, won the Coupe de France. They could list Zinedine Zidane, Patrick Vieira and Gaël Clichy among their alumni, and last played in Ligue 1 in 1997/98. They were having a decent season, lying third in National 3 despite a worrying hiccup – they'd lost three of their last five matches and won only once. And, like Genoa, they owed their existence to an Englishman. On 4 August 1902, Herbert Lowe and some friends created Association Sportive de Cannes. As with Genoa, some 200 miles to the east on the Italian Riviera, football was not the sole reason for the club's formation. Members also competed in athletics and swimming events before opting to concentrate solely on football.

A Scotsman was also influential in the history of Cannes. Billy Aitken, born in Peterhead on 2 February 1894, played 293 times for clubs as varied as Rangers, Norwich City, Newcastle United, Port Vale, Preston North End and Bideford Town. To move from the north Devon town of Bideford to manage Juventus seems surreal, but that's what Aitken did. Apparently, Juve owner Edoardo Agnelli agreed with Aitken's enthusiasm for the novel system then being played by Arsenal under Herbert Chapman. The latter's 'WM' formation, named after the letters because the players resembled them if set out on a diagram (it can also be described as a 3-2-2-3 formation), led to an early-1930s league title and FA Cup success for Arsenal, and by the late 1930s it had been adopted by most English clubs. Playing the WM under Aitken, Juventus came third in the Italian league in 1929/30. Aitken then joined Cannes and was part of the side that beat FC Roubaix 1-0 in the 1932 Coupe de France. He remained player-manager of *Les Dragons* for two years, before spells with Stade de Reims and, back on the French Riviera, FC Antibes.

When I was driving into Cannes for the first time, searching for the Stade Pierre de Coubertin, Aitken flitted in and out of my thoughts. Apparently he worked as a defence contractor during the Second World War for engineering conglomerate Vickers-Armstrongs. After the war he had further coaching stints abroad, in Belgium and Norway, before settling in Tyne and Wear and working for a wine and spirits distributor. He died in 1973, and aside from such a peripatetic career was noted for one particular trick: the seal dribble.

The seal dribble's most famous exponent has to be Kerlon Moura Souza of Brazil. Kerlon, hailed as a *wunderkind* in his early years as a youth player in Brazil in the early 2000s, became notorious for one of football's most esoteric tricks – flicking the ball up while running, controlling it momentarily on his forehead and then running past opponents while juggling the ball on his head. It's an outrageous manoeuvre, worse even than a nutmeg in its ability to humiliate whoever it bypasses. Kerlon got a lot of stick for it, but as he told *Globoesporte*, 'Even knowing that I would suffer a foul or a violent challenge, I still tried it, flicking the ball up in the air and travelling metres with the ball on my head, not letting it drop. That was the style of my football: irreverent, with lots of joy.'

Footage online shows Kerlon being battered by defenders for the seal dribble, most notoriously when playing in Brazil for Cruzeiro against Atlético Mineiro in the Belo Horizonte city derby. Mineiro's Dyego Coelho acted quickly to halt a Kerlon seal dribble in its tracks – by elbowing him in the face. Coelho got his marching orders and a 120-day ban. Other footage shows Kerlon, a slimline 5ft 6in, embarking on the seal dribble in a crowded midfield or wide on the wing, usually beating two or three players with it before being clattered to the turf. Predictably, he picked up a lot of injuries, which may be why he retired, aged 29, having never realised his potential. But as Dante Clarke writes on *Planet Football*, Kerlon had no regrets. Clarke quotes a Kerlon line to *Globoesporte*, 'Guided by my greatest partner and friend, my father, we created a skill that had never been seen before. I did it in big moments, both for Brazil and for

Cruzeiro, even in a big derby at a packed Mineirao.' And Clarke concludes:

'And his pride is well placed. Few players can do something genuinely original and inventive on a football pitch.

'Kerlon might not have turned out to be the superstar many predicted, but nobody will ever be able to take his ingenious seal dribble away from him.'

Except that Billy Aitken, also slightly built and 5ft 6in, was known to run along the touchline doing the seal dribble too.

I was fascinated by Aitken. To move from Bideford Town to manage Juventus is one thing. To win the Coupe de France is another. To pioneer the ultimate fancy dan move, in the 1920s, put him in the stratosphere.

I felt sure Aitken would have appreciated the talents of Elyes Ayéche. My own wish to see him play again had been given a boost by a minor miracle, so far as I was concerned: I'd played football a few days earlier. Just five-a-side, but my knee had held up and it was a lovely run-about. I couldn't believe it. I'd been the old bloke on the pitch for the past few years, but the twin developments of moving to France (where there didn't seem to be a local crew up for football) and a partial meniscectomy on my right knee put paid to all thoughts of carrying on. I should have known better on one of these points: there is always a local crew who are up for football. Doumé proved to be the organiser. And those gentle runs in England over Christmas had continued in France. I was even older, and as mobile as a lamp-post, but I loved playing football and was as thrilled as a 12-year-old selected for the first team to be back. Now, this evening, here we were in Cannes, to see the extraordinary Ayéche again.

But Ayéche would not be featuring in this 6pm fixture. Needless to say, this was not deduced by reading a programme. As usual, there were none to be seen. But Ayéche wasn't on the pitch, that was for sure. Perhaps the yellow card he'd received in the Rousset game meant he was now suspended. It was impossible to know. There is not a surfeit of information on games down in the National 3; in contrast to our trips to places like Genoa, Nice, Monaco and Marseille, a quick Google search on one's phone yielded next to nothing. But everything we needed to know was playing out very clearly on the pitch.

Villefranche SJB, despite playing some nice football in the first ten to 15 minutes, were being totally outclassed. Somehow, they hung on until the 39th minute, when 20-year-old striker Stanislas Kielt put Cannes a goal up. Kielt added a second on the stroke of half-time. Villefranche's goalkeeper, Kevin Blois, was having a shocker, deciding to punch the ball when he could catch it, looking suspect for every cross and often out of position. John and I shook our heads at half-time. Without Ayéche, and with their goalkeeper taking the word 'mercurial' into uncharted territory, Villefranche SJB had no chance. Bizarrely, Blois had a much better game in the second half, but his side still conceded another three goals.

It was a rout. The Stade Pierre Coubertin holds 10,000; sadly for AS Cannes, I'd say only 800 to 1,000 were there to see *Les Cannois* win so convincingly. A long way from the record gate, against Marseille on 31 July 1994, when 17,401 people crammed into the half-formed stadium.

It's a strange place, one of the most peculiar grounds I've ever visited. Located a skip and a jump from Cannes La Bocca train station, a few miles from central Cannes and a ten-minute walk from the Mediterranean, it feels at once grand and decrepit. On the eastern side of the pitch there is a large two-tier covered stand, with the lower-tier seats bearing the name, in red, of AS Cannes. It's greying and worn, but, maybe because its roof angles skywards, seems tall and imposing. To the west, there is a smaller, single-tier stand. But behind the goals, there is nothing. The north and south end stands were either never built, or they've been destroyed. Given the expanse of concrete behind each goal, I'd put money on the stands having been taken down. Something must have been there, once upon a time. Outside the stadium, on the western side, is a car park, but it somehow feels more like a derelict building site than a place to stow one's vehicle.

What would Pierre de Coubertin, educator, historian, founder of the International Olympic Committee and father of the modern Olympic Games, make of the stadium that bears his name? Or of the wild-looking, long-haired, deeply tanned, middle-aged and scruffy man who walked among the fans in the single-tier stand before the game, dispensing, gratis, honey-roasted peanuts? De Coubertin does not lack for stadia with his name: they're all over France. But this one – and with no offence to the peanut man (whose offerings were delicious) – could do with a makeover.

'*Cannes surclasse le VSJB*,' proclaimed *Nice-Matin* the following day. 'Cannes out-class Villefranche SJB.' There's no argument when you've been on the receiving end of a 5-0 defeat. *Nice-Matin* rubbed it in a bit in the final paragraph of its match report, which read:

'Quant au VSJB, il reste toujours scotché (et décroché) a l'avant-dernière place synonyme de relégation.'

At least, though, the mini-ultras weren't present to see their side's hammering, to walk away in the nippy night air and contemplate VSJB's being glued to the relegation zone. Despite graffiti emblazoned in red on a wall on the exterior of the western stand, calling for *'Liberté pour les ultras'*, VSJB's excitable teen and pre-teen contingent hadn't made it for this local derby. There would be no bullfighters' dance as we drove out of the car park. A shame, but it was an evening game: their parents must have told them it was too late to be out.

* * *

The flashing blue lights meant only one thing. On the slip road as the A709 heads into Montpellier, I had to pull over.

Stupid. Right at the end of a four-hour drive from Menton, I'd let my speed drift upwards. I was tired. I just wanted to get to my hotel. There was no other traffic on the road. No excuse. And an unmarked French police car had just parked behind my hire car (I couldn't take our own car because Caroline needed it), its two officers had climbed out of their seats and were now walking towards me.

I wound down the window. *'Bonsoir,'* I said. One of them said nothing, the other seemed to toy with the concept of being friendly. 'Where are you going?' he asked. *'Je vais bavarder à Stephy Mavididi, le joueur de football,'* was my reply, in less than correct French. He repeated his question. I then said I was a journalist, despatched to interview Mavididi for *The Times*. This was true. I'd suggested an interview with Mavididi to the sports desk and they'd said yes. Again, the officer asked where I was going, asking also if I was in a hire car. Yes, it's a hire car, I said. But where are you going, asked the officer, and now he wanted to see my driving licence too.

'Ah, *désolée monsieur*! Here is my licence, and I am on my way to the Holiday Inn hotel.'

'This is an English licence?'

'Yes.'

'And you are in a hire car?'

'Yes.'

'How long will you be here for?'

'Perhaps two or three days. I will be interviewing Stephy Mavididi for *The Times*. Do you know him?'

At roughly this point the officer grew tired of my French and switched to near-perfect English.

'Do you know why we have stopped you?' he asked.

'Er, *trop vitesse*?' I said.

'Yes. You were driving at 150kmh. The limit was 130kmh for much of the road, but then it became 90kmh before this turning. You were doing 150kmh in a 90kmh zone.'

I made profuse apologies. I told them I was tired. My hotel was not far. It had been a long drive. But that was no excuse. I was sorry. Very sorry.

The officer half-smiled. He paused for a very long time. He looked at his colleague. His colleague looked at him. I can only think they communicated telepathically, because neither words nor even facial expressions occurred. Eventually, the English-speaking officer spoke. 'It is your lucky night,' he said. 'Drive slowly from now on.'

I drove at a snail's pace through Montpellier's outlier roads, and wondered: had announcing that I'd be interviewing Mavididi done the trick? Were the officers fans of *La Paillade*? Or was it too much hassle to fine an Englishman driving a hire car, with an English licence?

The next day I rose early and drove even more slowly to Montpellier's training ground. I've interviewed footballers in the past, and the drill is always the same: there's a lot of waiting. You wait for a training game to finish, you wait for the post-match debriefing, you wait for the player to have some treatment from the physio. Or, as happened when I was to interview Ian Holloway, also for *The Times*, at QPR's training ground, there's a misunderstanding between journalist and club press officer, and despite gaining entry to the training ground no one knows you're there. You wait, and wait, and wait, not wanting to interrupt a man such as Holloway, a player I'd liked a lot when he was alongside Ray Wilkins in the QPR midfield and who was now the club's manager. Finally, I plucked up the courage to tell Holloway who I was and why I was there. He was charm itself, incredibly apologetic about what had turned into a three-hour wait and generous with his time when he'd have doubtless quite liked to have gone home and called it a day.

Mavididi was cut from the same cloth. I didn't have to wait three hours to talk to him but had to wait for perhaps an hour before he appeared. 'Sorry, really sorry,' he said. 'I had to get my knee checked out, got a slight knock in training.' We had a good chat. Mavididi is likeable, modest

The old town of Menton, the port of Garavan and Italy

The magical Stan Bowles

The Olympic arches of the Stade Louis II

No confusion in the beautiful lines of the Stadio Luigi Ferraris

he Sampdoria faithful

An Englishman in France: Stephy Mavididi

e Allianz Riviera Stadium. What could possibly go wrong?

Marseille's ultras are among the most passionate in the world – but it wasn't their day when Brest came to town

Cap Ferrat: not a typical football town

A handful all night long – Adama Traoré shoots again during the La Liga match between RCD Espanyol and Barcelona at RCDE Stadium on 13 February 2022

Still a class apart but is he happy? Lionel Messi in action for Paris Saint-Germain against Nice in the Allianz Riviera Stadium on 5 March 2022

A lesser known José Mourinho – in goal at the Game for Grenfell

Still in Serie A: Spezia Calcio

The Grecians go up. And they still sell programmes in obvious places – unlike just about every Mediterranean football club

There are some squishy tomatoes somewhere: AEK Athens fans get ready to rumble

Back in Brumano, Italy

and genuine. I admired his pluck in moving abroad, first to Italy and then to France. His French was good and, if it was clear he yearned to star one day in the Premier League, he'd made a good life for himself in the south of France. He was settled with a French girlfriend, enjoyed the weather (it had been the third-hottest January in the south of France since 1958), and headed to the beach for downtime when he could. Montpellier was a lot quieter than London, but he'd grown used to its slower pace.

One of a select club of English footballers playing on the continent, arguably Mavididi is the most successful of those in France. They include Colchester-born, France-bred (from the age of four) goalkeeper Etienne Green, who plays for Saint-Étienne (a great club with a joint-record of ten Ligue 1 titles who were then in the top flight, but would be relegated by the end of the season); former Crystal Palace youth player Levi Lukema, who signed for Ligue 2's Troyes on 28 July 2020 (helping them win the Ligue 2 title in 2020/21), and Rhys Evitt-Healey, an ex-Cardiff City striker who has been with Ligue 2's Toulouse since August 2020 (Evitt-Healey's goals would help take Toulouse to promotion as champions in 2021/22).

A couple of weeks after my trip to Montpellier, *The Times* ran my interview with Mavididi:

Mavididi relishing key role for Montpellier as club push for Europe

Striker counts Thierry Henry as a mentor and was first Englishman to play for Juventus in 27 years

Stephy Mavididi is having a good season. With eight goals to his name, the 23-year-old striker, born in Derby and brought up in east London, is thriving at Montpellier, helping the Ligue 1 side make a serious push for European competition next season.

'We don't talk about Europe, and we haven't set it as a target,' says Montpellier's number ten. 'But we know there's talk among the fans, and it's great that the club is in contention.'

Montpellier's strong first half of the season foundered a little on their last outing, a Coupe de France defeat on penalties to Mediterranean rivals Marseille. But the preceding weekend Mavididi was on fire, netting twice as Montpellier beat Monaco 3-2 to move into sixth place in the league. Both his goals were textbook finishes which would have delighted Mavididi's mentor, one Thierry Henry.

'Henry was a huge influence on me,' says Mavididi, whose 16-year-old brother Shaun is on Newcastle's books. 'He helped me massively when I was at Arsenal, and then later, when I was looking to move from Juventus.'

Mavididi joined Arsenal when he was 12, after a period with Southend United and much-respected east London grassroots club Rippleway. Football was in his blood from day one. 'I just loved it, loved the feeling of kicking a ball as soon as I could walk. I started training when I was three or four.' Dedicated even before he'd reached double figures, the young Mavididi would train, stay behind to watch training sessions and games involving older players, then train again.

He took the same level of commitment to Arsenal. 'Arsène Wenger was in charge, and Steve Bould was his assistant. There was a great atmosphere there.

Everyone had the same vision. Everyone wanted to play football.'

Chief among them, of course, Henry. The prolific French international would have been proud of Mavididi's perfect holding of the line before slipping into space, to turn and take a pass on his right foot. Bang, and the ball was in the top-right corner; 3-2 to Montpellier, and delirium among the majority of the fans in the 32,900-seater Stade de la Mosson.

Ligue 1 suits Mavididi's game. Six foot, lean and fast, he's blessed with exceptional control. 'It's a very technical league,' he says. 'All the players are happy with the ball at their feet. Even in the lower leagues in Italy and France, you won't see a defender smash the ball away. They always look to play their way out of trouble. It's not as fast as the Premier League, but it's a great league to play in.'

And in Teji Savanier, Mavididi is fortunate to work with one of the best playmakers in France. Montpellier's captain has been on breathtaking form this season, so much so that there are calls for him be capped by the national side. 'Teji is brilliant, one of the very best,' says Mavididi. 'He represented France's Olympic team and there's stiff competition for his position in the French team, but he's definitely rubbing shoulders with them.'

Savanier was born in Montpellier, whose football team has a solitary Ligue 1 title to its name, bagged in 2011/12. Laurent Blanc, one of French football's icons, made 243 appearances for the club, while Eric Cantona netted ten times in 33 games while on loan in the 1989/90 season. Mavididi himself has encountered first-hand one of modern football's greats – Cristiano Ronaldo, whom he met during his spell at Juventus.

'I'd had some loan spells at Charlton and Preston while I was at Arsenal, and loved my time there, but when Juventus came calling I couldn't say no,' recalls Mavididi. 'Juve is a huge club. They'd decided to enter a reserve team in Serie C, and aim for Serie B. I decided to give it my all, to play for the B team and try and break through into the first team.'

Mavididi became close to Ronaldo, marvelling at, and learning from, his commitment to staying in shape as much as his ability. 'What he does off field keeps him on it,' he says. He went on to play in 32 games for Juve's Serie C team, training regularly with the first team and making his debut in Serie A when he came on as a substitute in a defeat to Ferrara SPAL. In the next game, Juventus wrapped up the title – and Mavididi became the first Englishman to play for the Old Lady since David Platt, in 1992.

Title celebrations were accompanied by sadness. Mavididi's father passed away around the same time, and Mavididi spent some six weeks away from the club. On his return, it was clear Mavididi wasn't to be in the reckoning for the first team. Enter, again, Henry, with the recommendation that he sign on loan for Dijon. Mavididi scored five times before Covid curtailed the season.

In June 2020, Mavididi signed for Montpellier in a €6.3m deal. The fans have taken to him, he's learned to speak French to a good level, and life in the south of France is good. 'The beaches, the sunshine, the weather – there's a great vibe here,' as he puts it.

But Mavididi's sights are set on a return to England. 'It's no secret that I want to play in the Premier League. It's the best league in the world.' And, of course, he'd like to add to his many England Under-17 to Under-20 appearances with a full cap.

What price a transfer someday soon to Newcastle, where his brother Shaun is learning his trade? Or maybe, if they're promoted to the Premier League this season, to QPR, whose in-form Chris Willock is Mavididi's best friend?

Mavididi laughs. 'We'll see,' he says. And then he's off, to train and train again.

* * *

Montpellier, to talk to Mavididi and to see *La Paillade's* home game against Lens, was an excursion away from the French and Italian Rivieras. So was the trip to Nîmes. Not quite Riviera football. Not quite Mediterranean, either, for Nîmes. A slightly divergent way to test my theory, or, perhaps, a legitimate if left-field compare and contrast exercise. Athens had been in my sights from the off. I still planned to go there, to see AEK Athens, to make the trek by way of my own obscure homage to Stan Bowles. I had no idea when I would be able to do this, or if it would really happen.

I made two other sorties to matches away from the French and Italian Rivieras. Both were to Barcelona.

The first was for *El Clásico*, the match between FC Barcelona and Real Madrid. This edition was at Camp Nou on 24 October, 2021. The second was to watch RCD Espanyol v Barcelona on Sunday, 13 February.

It was Eric, the magical programme procurer at Montpellier v Lens, who put me in mind of *El Clásico*. Eric's job took him to various motor racing circuits in Europe. He was a little tired of the travel, mainly because of the endless Covid tests. But one trip took him to Barcelona, a city he raved about, 'It's got everything. Festivals all the time, it's by the sea, the quality of life there is fantastic.' I asked how easy it was to get to. 'It's a one-hour flight from Nice.'

One hour! I'd be there in no time. I'd always wanted to see *El Clásico,* either at the Bernabéu, Real Madrid's stadium, or at Barça's Camp Nou. Fabled stadia, fabled clubs. And Fred Grace, an English film-maker who I knew through Saturday five-a-side games in London, lived in Barcelona. Fred had never been to a *Clásico* either. We were as excited as ten-year-olds when we met in a bar near Camp Nou, with a Spanish friend of Fred's called David. He was a proud member of the *culés*, the name by which Barcelona fans are known, if also a despondent one. 'The team is in transition,' he told us, wearily. 'They are not playing well.' David was not optimistic for his team. 'We miss Messi,' he said. 'I think it will be a draw today.'

The pre-match atmosphere was electric. I'd walked from my hotel in the city centre to Camp Nou, not bothering to look at a map and instead following the hordes in their Barça colours. Now, in a crowded bar some 300 yards from the stadium, the noise was so loud I had to strain to hear Fred and David. *Culés* around us were singing, chanting, clapping, roaring – making every sound imaginable. We could hear the songs of those inside Camp Nou too. Firecrackers and flares were going off every minute. The boom of one firecracker as we made our way to the turnstiles made me jump.

Our seats were high in Lateral 3 Superior off Carrer de la Maternitat. In other words, we were up in the gods. Every football fan has read of Camp Nou and seen images of the 99,354-capacity stadium on television, but nothing prepares you for the experience of being there. The largest stadium in Spain and Europe – home to FC Barcelona since 1957 – is astounding. That it's been used to host a mass congregation, by Pope John Paul II on 17 November 1982, is apt. This is a vast, uncovered, open-air place of wonderment, of devotion, of celebration. The Pope's congregation saw 121,500 troop into Camp Nou; its record attendance for a football match is just short of that figure, with 120,000 present for the 1986 European Cup quarter-final between Barcelona and Juventus.

Days before my *Clásico,* Barcelona released plans to renovate Camp Nou, president Joan Laporta promising a 'safer stadium with better entrances' and the construction of a roof that would cover every seat. Despite the club being £1.15bn in debt, Laporta insisted the new 90,000-seater stadium would be 'at the avant garde of technology'. Seats would be bigger, there'd be new VIP areas, and 'sustainability [would be] at the DNA of the project': solar panels would be installed, there'd be geothermal energy and, underground and out of sight, a new water recycling system placed beneath the pitch. It was all part of the 'Espai Barça' makeover, an 18-acre upgrade to both Camp Nou and its surrounds.

It sounded great, but how would Barcelona afford it? The club was in turmoil. Debt and lack of cashflow meant that Lionel Messi, club captain and, probably, the greatest number ten the world has ever seen, had left for Paris Saint-Germain a few months earlier, signing a two-year deal on 10 August. For the flight from Nice to Barcelona I'd read some of Simon Kuper's *Barça: The Inside Story of the World's Greatest Football Club*. Kuper loves Barça; he also loves Johan Cruyff, the man behind the metamorphosis from 'a club of losers in a decrepit provincial city' to all-conquering footballing giant. But he's an objective journalist, too. His closing chapters, in a section called 'The Cathedral Crumbles', spare no blushes in chronicling how the mighty had fallen, and may yet fall further, because of financial mismanagement, poor transfer market dealings, ageing stars and *Messidependenica* – over-reliance on the sublime Messi, who cried when announcing his departure. As a senior club official told Kuper, 'After Messi you see the desert, you see darkness.'

Fred and I were surprised by how much we could see of the action, all the way back in one of the top tiers. Or rather, at how well we could discern the players. Fred also surprised me with a linguistic correction. 'It's not the "Nu" Camp,' he said. 'It's pronounced the "Now" Camp, or, as they say here, Camp "Now".' The previous night he'd got chatting to one of Barça's former doctors. 'He had some amazing stories,' said Fred. 'I'd love to make a film about him.'

Fred felt there was room for hope in the form of Ansu Fati, who'd been with Barça since he was ten. Now 18, Fati had stepped up to the plate, taking Messi's vacant number ten shirt. 'The locals say he's amazing, young but amazing. Maybe the next Messi.' A tall order, and although he showed some deft touches this was not to be the day Fati achieved a standing ovation from even the away fans – as happened to English winger Laurie Cunningham, fresh from West Bromwich Albion, when he dazzled in Real's 2-0 *Clásico* win at Camp Nou in 1980. Cunningham helped win the game, and won over the locals too, but their discontent would only grow as this game went on. Barça were not poor, but they were not great either. David Alaba broke the deadlock for Real Madrid in the 32nd minute; Lucas Vázquez scored from close range to kill off the hosts three minutes into added time. Barça nicked a consolation goal three minutes later thanks to Sergio Agüero's first goal for the club, but no one could say the visitors didn't deserve their win. I told Fred I hoped he got to make his film about the Barcelona doctor. '*Doctor Now*, for the title?'

But pity Barcelona. They weren't as close to my heart as they were to Kuper's, but I'd always had a soft spot for them. Cruyff and Messi were just two of a multitude of players that it was a pure delight to watch. In whatever year, for whatever manager, the football they played was breathtaking. Take your pick from Rivaldo, Pep Guardiola, Andrés Iniesta, Xavi, Ronaldinho, Luís Figo, Samuel Eto'o – the list seems endless. Bliss on the pitch, every time. Now the club resembled a once great but ageing boxer, still capable, still dangerous, but likely to be beaten by the younger, fitter man.

Away to our left, as we stood up to leave, I saw the sea. It wasn't as close as for the games I'd seen at Monaco, Menton or Sanremo, but there it was, the blue of the Mediterranean, occasional whitecaps underneath a layer of soft white haze. It'd be a shame when the roof was installed – assuming Barça found the money to build one. Everyone likes a sea view. Then I remembered what Dom and the English lads I'd met at the Stade Louis II told me, of their trip to Camp Nou. The heavens had opened. 'We got absolutely soaked,' said Dom. 'There's no cover there at all.'

True. But on my second visit to Barcelona I saw more of the city, even managing a trip to the beach, before heading to the RCDE Stadium for RCD Espanyol v Barcelona on 13 February. The most-played derby in La Liga is easily in the top five games I've ever seen. And this, a long weekend in Barcelona, got me thinking again about the influence of the Mediterranean on football. Or, perhaps more accurately, the effect of living in a Mediterranean city on football. For this time, in Barcelona with Caroline and Maud, and with John and Helén and their children there too, we did the usual tourist things: getting cabs to the Sagrada Familia, going to the zoo, eating out in restaurants in pretty little squares, ambling around the Old Town, braving the apparently ubiquitous pickpockets of La Rambla (our pockets were unpicked); and also some less usual things, like pondering how George Orwell Square got its name and who designed the classical lines of the Barcelona França railway station and even whether, as someone bizarrely told me, Barcelona really is a 'kinky' city (we happened upon no evidence).

Wherever we went, there was music. There was a gathering of some kind. There were festivals. One we stumbled into seemed to be for the city's drummers. On and on they marched, snaking through street after street, drumming, blowing whistles, singing. It was a Saturday and there were as many children in school uniforms as adults in carnivalesque clothing. Maud was fascinated. We were all swept up in it. There was joy everywhere.

If you live in a city like Barcelona, whether as a football fan or player, isn't this joy infectious? I think so – but Barcelona also taught me that despair can be catching, too.

Outside the 40,000 all-seater RCDE Stadium, as John, Fred and I ate pasta in a restaurant nearby, there were no harbingers of impending doom. We were three expat English football fans, looking forward to a new experience. Even Fred, the local, hadn't been to Espanyol's ground. We knew little about it, save that it was relatively new, having been officially opened in 2009 with a friendly against Liverpool (Espanyol won 3-0). Fred had heard it was a good ground, with the stands close to the pitch and therefore, for sell-out games, a cracking atmosphere.

I knew the *Derbi Barceloni* was La Liga's most-played derby, though also its most one-sided: Barcelona have won nearly three times as many of the encounters as Espanyol, including the one and only all-Catalan Copa del Rey Final in 1957. John wondered if a political subtext underpinned the fixture, Barça the beacon for the Catalan independence movement, Espanyol supposedly more compliant with centrist Spain. I recalled a story from a few years back, of Espanyol fans making the trek to Scotland for a Rangers v Aberdeen game. Some 20 or so waved Espanyol flags in a crowd of 50,000 at Ibrox, and told the *Daily Record*'s Gary Armstrong, 'We feel Espanyol are mirrored with Rangers in terms of the economic situation, but also because of the atmosphere, loyalty, passion and the colour blue that both teams share.' They also suggested Barça and Celtic shared the same reciprocal affection, but Joan Collet, former CEO of Espanyol, gave a more nuanced account in a 2016 interview with Rafel Bagot of *Metropolitan Barcelona*. As Collet told Bagot:

'We have to recognise that Espanyol exists side by side with a very big club, a world monster, FC Barcelona, and it's not easy to co-exist. The rivalry that is present in schools, on the street and at work, is naturally difficult. Quite difficult. But, well, we're proud of our team and I understand that lots of aficionados and tourists that come here have more feelings for Barcelona, because they're the team that wins.'

But as Bagot wrote: 'Furthermore, to be a *perico* – which means parakeet and is the name given to Espanyol fans as well as being the team's mascot – is often associated with a Spanish ideology and being Spanish, which contrasts with the nationalist feeling that Catalunya has with respect to Spain.

Since childhood, Collet has felt that he has gone against the tide.

'But I didn't feel this by myself. I've been made to feel it. The club has been badly treated throughout history and by the media. I'm from a town and the Espanyol supporters in my town, like in many others, are Catalans; we speak Catalan and we live in Catalan. We are from this land. I grew up hearing that Espanyol is a fascist team, a military team, a team followed by immigrants who had arrived from the rest of Spain and I couldn't understand it. The Espanyol that I had lived, the one that I knew, wasn't the one that they were describing.'

There was another memorable quote in Bagot's piece. He spoke to Quim Torrecillas, a lawyer from Blanes on the Costa Brava, who said:

"In Catalunya, we have to support Espanyol. To be a Barça fan is very easy. To follow Espanyol is to be the little shop owner, the small businessman … the person who doesn't want to have it all and only wants what he truly deserves from the effort he makes in his everyday life. This is what identifies Espanyol and also the way Catalans are. It's really *"La força d'un sentiment"* ("The strength of a feeling").'

Before the game, we only dimly apprehended any of this. It was that evening, back in my hotel, when I came across Bagot's piece. I couldn't sleep – the feeling of upset was too great – so I typed 'Espanyol' into Google. The game I'd just seen was as good as any I'd watched live. Its nearest competitor was QPR 2 Liverpool 2 in the FA Cup quarter-final in 1990. I'd been in the East Paddock, rapt throughout, terrified every time John Barnes had the ball, desperate for some magic by our latest classy number ten (United States international Roy Wegerle), heart in my mouth when Ian Rush put Liverpool 2-1 ahead with ten minutes to go, ecstatic when Simon Barker levelled the tie in the final minutes. Barker was my man of the match in a pulsating game that I'd never forgotten, not just because this was one of QPR's better sides (David Bardsley at right-back, David Seaman in goal, the late, great Alan McDonald at centre-half, Ray Wilkins pulling the strings and scoring our fine first goal, Andy Sinton, now club ambassador, as neat and smart as ever … I could go on) but because of the hypnotic ebb and flow of the football. You couldn't take your eyes off it. Espanyol v Barcelona had been as good, and I warmed to the idea of not wanting it all, of *La força d'un sentiment*. There was something very QPR about it.

Inside the RCDE Stadium, the ripples to west London only intensified. The ground was packed, with just about every fan singing as they held aloft a blue and white scarf. Fred was right – the RCDE is a compact stadium, larger than Loftus Road (most places are) but likewise the kind of place that generates a wild, manic, irresistible energy. Neutral before the game, it took all of a minute for Fred, John and I to plump for the underdogs. Our seats were behind the goal at the northern end, in the eye of a storm of *perico* ferocity. It was as if we'd wandered into another Barcelona street festival. There was nothing for it but to embrace the passion.

Which quickly took a dive: inside two minutes, Pedri turned in a cross from Jordi Alba. Same old, same old: Espanyol hadn't won this fixture since 2007. They'd never won it inside the RCDE Stadium. They went into the game with just one win in six, to Barcelona's four wins and two draws in their past six outings. Barcelona, whose motto is '*Més que un club*' ('more than a club'), had got back to winning ways since the Real Madrid reverse. Barça was, indeed, more than a club. It was an institution, a symbol, a repository of hope for a nation that wasn't a nation, a unique collective of talent and skill and vision. It was Collet's 'world monster', and the stage was set for a pleasing meal at the expense of its inferior poor relation.

Espanyol's fans rallied. They had to. Not only were their team a goal down, Adama Traoré, for all the world looking more like an Olympic 100m sprinter than a Wolves winger on loan to Barcelona, was a one-man demolition team. Assisted by Ronald Araüjo and Alba, he was just off target with two left-foot shots, but then, played in by Gavi (just 17 and another of Barça's bright young things), he fired an Exocet missile of a right-footed volley goalbound. It was met by a fine block from Espanyol goalkeeper Diego López, but Traoré was a revelation. He had superb technique, excellent vision and could pass perfectly. He was strong, powerful and blisteringly quick. Espanyol's defenders couldn't get near him – and Fred fancied he knew the reason why. It wasn't just Traoré's pace.

'The physios cover his arms in grease before each game,' said Fred. 'It's to stop defenders grabbing him.'

For grease, read baby oil. Wolves manager Nuno Espírito Santo confirmed as much towards the end of the 2020/21 season. Ahead of an away game at Manchester City, he told a press conference: 'I thought it was honestly a fantastic idea by the medical department because it came from the injury that he had with his shoulder. That was caused basically because of holding of his arm and creating this strong impact on his shoulder and he got injured from that.

'It's very hard to stop Adama, and that [baby oil] avoids that situation. He becomes more slippery, so we get the advantage of his speed and talent. It was an option to avoid it, and from then on, he's kept on doing it and it's good.'

The injury to which Santo referred was a dislocated shoulder. A four-times dislocated shoulder, at that. Apparently, it would pop out because defenders would wrench Traoré's arms to try and stop the Spanish international, or, at least, slow him down. The speed at which he would be travelling when this happened created enough force for the shoulder to free itself of its socket. Remarkably, on one occasion, in a game at Sheffield

United, Traoré had soldiered on for 77 minutes before being replaced.

If asked individually what they felt about a player for the national team suffering recurrent shoulder dislocations, somewhere other than the RCDE Stadium, Espanyol's fans would doubtless have been sympathetic. Tonight, it was a fair bet they didn't care – or maybe even sneakily hoped the medical staff had left the baby oil at Camp Nou, so that a discreet tug by Adrià Pedrosa or Aleix Vidal might lead to poor Traoré departing the pitch, à la Bryan Robson in the 1986 World Cup in Mexico.

Undeterred by the early setback, undaunted by Traoré, they sang and waved their flags and chanted. Anyone arriving late would never have guessed they were a goal down. On the advent of the 21st minute, they clapped for a whole 60 seconds in honour of club hero Daniel Jarque, a product of the club's youth system who'd only ever played for Espanyol (as well as Spain's Under-17, Under-19, Under-20 and Under-21 teams) before he died of a heart attack, aged just 26, on 8 August 2009 in a hotel room in Florence during a pre-season tour.

Cesc Fàbregas was the first player to pay tribute to the man who wore Espanyol's number 21 shirt, a team-mate from the Spanish Under-21 side. He dedicated his second goal in Arsenal's 15 August 2009 6-1 thumping of Everton at Goodison Park to Jarque, who'd just been named Espanyol team captain – and whose girlfriend was seven months pregnant at the time of his death. Two months later, as Jarque's child was being born, scorer Iván Alonso also paid tribute to his former colleague in Espanyol's 2-1 victory over Málaga CF at the RCDE Stadium. The most prominent homage of all was by Andrés Iniesta in the 2010 FIFA World Cup Final. Iniesta scored the only goal of Spain's win over a vicious Dutch side in the 116th minute, whereupon he took off his shirt to reveal a vest with the words '*Dani Jarque siempre con nosotros*' ('Dani Jarque, always with us').

The clapping in the 21st minute was more than touching. It was more than stirring. It was contagious. Espanyol were right back in it, taking the fight to Barcelona and getting their just desserts in the 40th minute when midfielder Sergi Darder curled in a lovely, right-footed shot from just outside the area. It was one of those goals whose flight, because of where we were sitting, we could track all the way. A work of art.

The pace was relentless. It was the fastest game I'd seen anywhere along the Mediterranean coastline. Both sides gave as good as they got, Espanyol's fans seeming to have a peculiarly visceral dislike of Barça stalwart Gerard Piqué. He was booed every time he touched the ball, and while I don't speak Spanish I know a swear word when I hear one. A great many went Piqué's way. To be fair, he hadn't endeared himself to the Espanyol faithful when, in 2016, he had said, 'They call themselves the "marvellous minority", and they're in such a minority that they can't even fill their ground.'

Harsh, but true. The RCDE looked full the night we were there, but the attendance was 25,049. Still, no one who was there will ever forget the game. It saw a Barca goal disallowed for offside early in the second half, before Darder sent a perfect pass to Raúl de Thomás, who calmly beat Barca's keeper, Germany's Marc-André ter Stegen.

There were another 25 minutes to go. They went by in a flash, neither side flagging, both going at it hell for leather, Piqué still the target for abuse and eventually the recipient of a red card in the 92nd minute. Barca threw everything at the home side and yet Espanyol hung on. This would be a famous victory! John, Fred and I had been standing for most of the second half, urging on Espanyol. Now the end was in sight.

And then, despair. I'd known this emotion as a QPR fan. It was the first time I'd experienced it for another club. One that I'd barely even registered until tonight.

But, as the excellent Traoré sent in a cross from the right side of midfield, I knew. John and Fred knew. Everyone behind the goal knew. Luuk de Jong's header was going in. López got a hand to the ball but couldn't keep it out of the net.

It ended 2-2. The RCDE Stadium fell silent. We, the English contingent, could only say, 'No. No, no, no.' Espanyol's players were distraught. One or two were crying. Their fans looked desolate. It was how we felt too.

To tell any of Espanyol's fans that football is just a game, that it's just a bunch of people chasing a ball around, that's it somehow childish and unimportant – all of which have been put to me by the unconverted over the years – would have been like telling them the death of one of their parents didn't matter.

Earlier we'd talked up having a few beers after the game, some *vino tinto*, sampling the Barcelona nightlife. Now we filed out of the RCDE Stadium, among the forlorn. There'd be no party tonight.

10

March 2022

Messi Muttering

Chère supportrice, cher supporter,
C'est un soir de Coupe de France qui nous attend à
l'Allianz Riviera ce mardi !
L'OGC Nice reçoit le FC Versailles, pensionnaire
de N2, pour sa première demi-finale depuis
2010/11. Un grand rendez-vous qui débutera à
21h face au Petit Poucet de la compétition, auteur
d'un parcours remarquable qui l'a notamment vu
éliminer Toulouse, club de Ligue 2.

COMMUNICATIONS FROM OGC Nice were never less than upbeat. This one landed in my inbox on the day of Nice's Coupe de France semi-final tie against lowly Versailles on Tuesday, 1 March. I'd already bought tickets for this *grand rendez-vous*, one that had caught my eye thanks to both sides' cup runs. Nice had beaten Paris Saint-Germain in the round of 16, before despatching

Marseille 4-1 in the quarter-final. It was proving to be a fine season for new manager Christophe Galtier, who'd taken Lille to their fourth Ligue title in 2021. Two days after guiding Lille to championship success, Galtier was off. 'I simply have the deep belief that my time is up here,' he told *L'Equipe*. Somehow, I couldn't imagine an English manager citing his deep belief in the same way. On 28 June 2021, Galtier, who'd played as a defender for Marseille for much of his career, was installed as Nice's new manager. Described online as a 'journeyman' footballer, there was nothing pedestrian about Galtier's coaching. Alongside no less a figure than Carlo Ancelotti, he won the Best Manager of the Year award at the Trophées UNFP du Football in 2013. Now, as well as taking Nice to within a whisker of the Coupe de France Final, Galtier had them lying in third place in Ligue 1.

Perhaps, under Galtier, Nice were about to experience a new dawn, adding a fourth Coupe de France victory to those they'd bagged in 1952, 1954 and 1997. *Les Aiglons* were the first French club to achieve the league and cup double, in 1952, and had won the Ligue 1 championship a total of four times, all in the 1950s. Galtier's team were fluent, fast and potent. Amine Gouiri and Andy Delort had found their rhythm; Kluivert junior had scored a brace in the quarter-final thrashing of Marseille. They were in contention to claim a Champions League place by the end of the season.

But if Nice were nailed-on favourites against Versailles, their opponents weren't about to roll over. FC Versailles 78, a relative newcomer – the club was formed by the merger in 1989 of Racing Club Versailles and Companion Sports Versailles – were top of National 2. Managed by Youssef Chibhi, they were looking good for promotion beyond the fourth tier of French football for the first time in their history. They'd survived six rounds of the cup to get this far, beating Ligue 2 side Toulouse in the round of 16 before a penalty shoot-out quarter-final win over Bergerac. Maybe, just maybe, there'd be an upset tonight. *Le Petit Poucet* would prevail, as in the fairytale written by Charles Perrault as one of his *Histoires ou Contes du temps passé* (1697). Here, despite his tiny stature, Hop-o'-My-Thumb or Little Thumb uses his wits to defeat an ogre.

John and I made it to the Allianz Riviera in time for kick-off, though we were again too late to see Mèfi the eagle (who, I'd discovered, is female). The stadium was fizzing with excitement. In sharp contrast to the Covid-related minuscule crowd for our last game here, against Nantes (who were playing Monaco in the other Coupe de France semi-final), now there was a healthy attendance of 26,723. We were high up at the back of the northern stand, behind the goal, above the smattering of Versailles fans who'd made the long trek from the outskirts of Paris to Nice. Opposite us, behind the goal, the massed ranks of Nice's ultras in the Populaire Sud were in full voice. A strong smell of hashish wafted our way, from some Nice fans to our left. It hadn't mellowed them. They and the vast majority in the Allianz Riviera were going for it, the most popular chant being:

'*Qui ne saute pas n'est pas Niçois – hey!*'

Literally, this is translates as 'whoever isn't jumping isn't from Nice'. Perhaps the English equivalent is 'Stand up, if you hate (insert name of team)'. I prefer the continental approach. '*Qui ne saute pas*' was chanted at just about every game I went to in France, each set of fans adding their own identity. I heard versions in Italy and Spain too. It depends on the same sense of collective action as stand up, if you hate (well, Chelsea, if you're a QPR fan), but it's rhythmic, insistent, and fun. When the chant begins at a French game, you stand up and start jumping. If you're at a Marseille game, only a small minority will not be chanting and jumping. Less a chant, more of a dirge, the English 'Stand up, if you hate Chelsea' (or whoever) will only ever see the zealots rise from their seats and proclaim their hatred. Even some of them seem half-hearted. Perhaps hating another group of people is tiresome.

There was nothing to object to during this trip to the Allianz Riviera, still less anyone to hate. John and I inevitably gravitated to Versailles, the plucky underdogs – who'd originally been drawn at home. Unfortunately for FC Versailles 78, their humble 7,500-seater Stade Montbauron is close to Versailles' rarefied Avenue de Paris and the world-famous Château de Versailles. The latter and its complex of gardens, theatre, chapel and Royal Opera House was designated a UNESCO World Heritage site in 1979. This, and a centuries-old dictat that 'visible light sources' were banned from reaching the king's room, means that floodlights cannot be erected, still less turned on, at the Stade Montbauron. So if, for Espanyol, neighbours Barcelona are the 'world monster' that ensures they languish eternally in relative obscurity, FC Versailles 78 have a rather different kind of overbearing big brother. A palace.

The ban on floodlights meant Versailles had to scrabble around to see if they could host the semi-final at a stadium in Paris (just 12 miles away to the east). Paris Saint-Germain declined to make the Parc des Princes available and evidently the logistics became too painful all round, and so here they were, the hardworking, well-organised and physically fit men from National 2. And fit they had to be. Nice pummelled them in the first half, Amine Gouiri looking constantly dangerous but also, to Versailles' relief, a little profligate too. Not so in the second half. That Versailles made it to half-time with the score at 0-0 was hugely to their credit, but a slick one-two on the right wing led to a cross, which was expertly volleyed home by Gouiri. Versailles' players' heads went down. Nice pushed on, with Gouiri, who'd made his professional debut aged just 16 for Bordeaux, showing why he is so highly rated. He capped a fine game with a mazy dribble in the 73rd minute, beating three or four Versailles' men before unselfishly laying the ball into the path of Kasper Dolberg. The Denmark international, voted player of the year by Nice's fans in 2020, hit a left-footed shot low to the goalkeeper's right. Goal – and most of the plaudits, from fans and team-mates alike, went to Gouiri.

A few days later Gouiri would cheerfully tell *Nice-Matin* that no, he wasn't really a great fan of defending. '*Je suis attaquant, je ne sais pas tacler,*' he said. That brought a smile to my face. It's the sort of thing Stan would have said. It's what I used to say to every exasperated captain in the amateur Saturday and Sunday teams I played for. At least Gouiri and Stan could back it up with ridiculous skill, not to mention an audience. Or, as *Nice-Matin* paraphrased the 22-year-old from Bourgoin-Jaillieu, near Lyon:

'*Marquer et être en connexion avec le public, il n'y a rien de plus fort.*' 'Scoring and feeling that connection with the crowd, there's nothing better.'

The tie ended as a 2-0 win to Nice. *Les Aiglons* had booked their place in the final of the Coupe de France, as everyone knew they would. *Le Gym*, their other nickname given their establishment in 1904 as *Gymnaste Club de Nice*, were technically and physically superior to their opponents. Jim Ratcliffe, INEOS chairman, owner of Nice since August 2019 and serial contender for richest man in Britain (according to the *Sunday Times* Rich List), could go home to Monaco a happy man – if he'd been at the game, and wasn't elsewhere pursuing any of his plethora of other interests; was he in England, perhaps, heading to his other home in Hampshire?

For the football club which plays in the ever-darkening shadows of a palace, it'd had been a hard night's toil. To play against a team four tiers higher, at its ground and facing players of the quality of Gouiri, Dolberg, Thuram and Andy Delort, was too big an ask. But FC Versailles 78 would have their memories. Not just of an amazing cup run and playing at the noisy, rambunctious Allianz Riviera stadium, but of training ahead of the game at the French national team's base at Clairefontaine, of using AS Monaco's facilities while on the French Riviera, of the respectful applause from *Les Niçois* when the final whistle blew. They'd return to Versailles, some solely as footballers, two, at least, with jobs to manage as well. As Raphaël Jucobin reported for *Get French Football News*:

'Even though Versailles are technically an amateur club who play in a regionalised division, most of the squad earn their living solely from football. Some take other jobs on the side. Their 22-year-old captain, Maël Durand de Gevigney, is in the final year of a physiotherapy degree, while the midfielder Oussama Berkak works as an IT consultant.'

By the end of the season, FC Versailles 78 had done it. They won National 2 in style, eight points ahead of second-placed Lorient 2. They would play in the Championnat de France National (often referred to simply as 'the National') for the first time.

Nice weren't able to add to their tally of Coupe de France wins. In the final at the Stade de France in Paris on 7 May, Nantes beat them 1-0 to claim their own fourth success in the competition.

* * *

It took a long time to get back to Menton after Nice v Versailles. The traffic was backed up for miles around the Allianz Riviera; we walked through our doors in the early hours. This quibble aside, John and I had finally experienced a proper game in Nice. It would be wrong to co-opt this as a symbol, still less adopt it as some form of exorcism (at last, the Allianz Riviera is no longer cursed!), but around this time I also had a minor breakthrough in terms of quotidian French life. People had told me it would go like this – little moments when you go 'Ah, I get it now' – and they were right.

My conversational French was now OK. I could understand what Vincent, Blondine and Christel were saying when I was buying the bread in L'Amie du Pain. Not always – I still felt they spoke faster than an express train – but enough. We'd pass the time of day and have a conversation, cars flowing back and forth between France and Italy outside, people coming and going, cyclists especially, the Med gleaming across the road, L'Amie the heart of everything here on the Franco-Italian frontier. Covid had been at bay for a few months now, too. 'In France, they kiss on main street' went the Joni Mitchell song. Well, the locals weren't quite kissing as before, but people were socialising again. Caroline, Maud and I were getting out and about. My knee was fine and I was playing football once a week. I was swimming each day, cycling Maud to school, and enjoying the small steps forward in French that were happening. My accent left a lot to be desired, while Caroline's was excellent. Her French had come on in leaps and bounds; we were the same level now. Maud was at a dance school, beginning the preparations for an end-of-year performance in the Palais du Europe in central Menton. We'd made friends, had a community, had our routines. All under the ever-present sun of the Côte d'Azur.

Damn it, life was good in Menton.

But we'd made our decision. We'd be leaving by the end of the summer and moving inland to Wiltshire. Our house in Cornwall went on the market. Such is post-Covid property madness in the UK that we were offered the asking price almost immediately. The die was cast. Our house-sitters would move out. We'd fly back and pack up, probably two or three times before the eventual sale, which was set for May. On one trip, in early April, emotions ran high. Were we really selling our house and leaving

Cornwall? Looking out over the roofs of the houses of Penzance one morning when we woke up, to the sound of seagulls and the sight of the sea beyond, Caroline was in tears. We'd loved living here. The neighbours were great, we had loads of friends, my grown-up sons lived in Cornwall; an old dog had died in my arms in the sitting room and I'd buried her in the garden. It seemed, in a flash, that we'd gone to live in France, and now, nearly two years later, we were about to depart Cornwall for good. One minute we had one life, the next another. It felt as if we hadn't made the decisions, as if instead we were puppets, helpless as we were manoeuvred by a force we couldn't comprehend.

In the face of feelings like this, there is a guaranteed antidote. His name is John O'Hare.

John is a man for whom the expression 'larger than life' could have been invented. He is large. Not a giant, but I struggle to think of anyone in Menton who's got the same frame. And if someone who is larger than life is someone who attracts a lot of attention, this is true of John. Not just because of his 6ft 4in height and proportionate body. No, John is larger than life because of his ready wit, infinite energy and ideas (he has a whiteboard in his office, listing idea after idea after idea) and his compulsive need to entertain.

'We need to describe ourselves for the podcast,' he once declared.

I told him I agreed.

'I'd like to be described as "Entertainer",' he said.

That was fine by me.

It's not that John is insensitive. Far from it. But he isn't one to overanalyse a given situation. Something either is, or it isn't. Better crack on with a joke than dwell on things.

In the midst of my growing confusion over where to call home, John cut to the chase. 'We're seeing Paris Saint-Germain tonight. That untidy player! Messi! Lionel Messi!' In other words: enjoy life, have a laugh and concentrate on the football.

* * *

It was good advice. After years of drooling over his exploits from afar, OGC Nice v Paris Saint-Germain on Saturday, 5 March meant I'd finally see Lionel Messi, the maestro, in the flesh. Messi had made a hesitant start to life in Paris, where he was contracted to remain until June 2023. There were rumours of discord in the dressing room, his family's struggles to learn French and adapt to Parisian ways, and even excessive partying. This had to be improbable, given how reserved and introverted Messi always seems. The accolades were certainly blind to the gossip, concentrating only on the statistics. Aged 34, over the calendar year Messi had helped Argentina win the Copa América (his first international honour). He'd also scored 40 goals in 2021/22 for Barcelona, four for Paris Saint-Germain and eight for Argentina. And so, to the chagrin of Bayern Munich and Poland striker Robert Lewandowski's agent, if not Lewandowski himself, Messi collected a record seventh Ballon d'Or on 29 November 2021. Lewandowski came second. Messi's seventh official ranking as the best footballer in the world put him two ahead of five-time winner and arch-rival Cristiano Ronaldo.

Perhaps, though, there was something in the rumours of parties. The day after the Ballon d'Or festivities, Messi missed training. As a PSG statement put it, 'Lionel Messi and [team-mate] Leandro Paredes did not participate in the training session today due to symptoms of gastroenteritis. A further check will be made tomorrow morning.' That sounded like PR-speak for a hangover. Regardless, it was clear Messi was struggling with fitness. Up to the Ballon d'Or evening, he'd featured in just seven of PSG's 15 Ligue 1 matches to date, completing only four.

The new year didn't signal a fresh start. On 2 January 2022, PSG confirmed Messi had tested positive for Covid. He had to miss two league games and one cup tie.

Still, the former Barça number ten had managed to rack up six assists since the turn of the year. He'd scored a few goals, and had a hat-trick of assists to his name when *Les Parisiens* beat Saint-Étienne 3-1 away from home the previous November.

But for every flash of form, there seemed to be a setback. For Lionel Messi – world superstar, conjuror, shy where Ronaldo was brash, Diego Maradona's self-appointed successor, scorer of 474 goals in 520 La Liga appearances for Barcelona – it had been a stop-start first few months at Paris Saint-Germain.

Chances were that Messi was inwardly questioning his move. Or, put more bluntly, that he was desperately missing Barcelona, the club he'd been with for more than 20 years.

Més que un club? For Messi, Barça was more than a club. It was his family.

* * *

'The lad wearing number 30's not bad, is he?'

John's height gave him a distinct advantage. Our seats were behind the goal among the Populaire Sud – 'the popular ultras', for John, as opposed to Nice's unpopular ones. We couldn't get anywhere near them. No one was sitting down, there was smoke from flares everywhere, fans were pushing and shoving, everyone was on their feet and no one was anywhere near their designated seat. We opted to stand behind the last row of seats. It was just about the only vantage point. Even then, as the game kicked off, there was a thick band of dark-grey smoke between us and the pitch, which, combined with the large banner held above their heads by a mass of the Populaire Sud, meant we'd be lucky if we caught the occasional glimpse of a player. On the banner were the words *'Per La Gloria De Nissa'*. It was the largest banner I'd seen at a game, and meant that even John, half a foot taller than me, was having trouble seeing anything. We tried moving around to our left. It was no good, the view was even worse.

Back we went, amid the ultras. By now scuffles were breaking out behind us on the concourse. For a moment, I thought the ultras were fighting among themselves, but then realised the police were the object of their ire. Commendably, they kept their cool, icily staring down the jostling, heckling *Niçois*, saying nothing, barely moving, hands clasped to their batons or pistol-butts but not, thankfully, doing anything with them.

It paid to keep an eye on what was going on behind us, but after a few minutes the smoke cleared, the banner was lowered and there he was, Lionel Messi, number 30 for PSG.

'Do you think he's got a future?' asked John.

A minute or two later, Messi made an immaculate, inch-perfect crossfield pass. He followed this by ghosting into space, untracked by any defenders – one of his signature moves – only for the ball not to come his way. Yes, he had a future. He was still a class apart. And then, nothing. Goalless at half-time, the runaway Ligue 1 leaders and would-be Coupe de France victors were cancelling each other out. PSG were without Kylian Mbappé, missing through suspension, but Mauricio Pochettino still had a line-up that featured Messi, Neymar, Ángel Di María, Marco Verrati and Gina Wijnaldum. Superstars all, and their team-mates were no slouches either. PSG were 15 points clear at the top of Ligue 1, and had the better record against Nice, who had managed just one win in their last 17 Ligue 1 outings against *Les Parisiens*. But Nice had knocked PSG out of the Coupe de France. Having lost 41 per cent of their league games at home against PSG – their worst percentage against a current Ligue 1 club – the cup win gave them belief. They were up for it, but the result of confidence versus class was stalemate. As Messi left the field for the break, his body language said it all. Head down, hand scratching his hair, movement a little too languid. He wasn't enjoying himself.

It was more of the same in the second half. Wisps of fog hung over the pitch, the Populaire Sud's *capos* kept the troops in voice, and a couple of ultras wandered up to John and me and asked us what we were doing. We showed them *Footy on the Med*'s website on our phones and told them we were making a podcast. One of them clapped John on the back. He told others nearby. Smiles all round. Relief, too, and not just for us: we realised the ultras thought we were undercover security or police officers. Not very subtle ones, given how blatant our equipment was. Nor very sophisticated ones either, given the looks that had come my way when I'd pulled out a wedge of papers to check some facts. But the Populaire Sud gave us a pass, and we'd found a spot from which we could see the action clearly. Our journey to the belly of the *Niçois* beast was working out fine – if only there'd been any action.

In truth, Nice v PSG was one of the most boring games of football I've ever seen. Maybe another factor in PSG's lacklustre performance was the club's coming midweek European Champions League tie against Real Madrid. Were the players saving themselves, doing just enough to keep Nice at bay? They were light years from what we'd hoped for and, indeed, expected. Messi declined to virtual invisibility by the end, Neymar was off the pace, Di María had surely played much better when he was at Manchester United.

It was almost as dull as the match that was my long-time winner of the Most Boring Game title: QPR v Wimbledon at Loftus Road on 29 August 1990. A crowd of some 9,000 suffered that late-summer day as the two sides seemed to compete for who could kick the ball the highest, or most aimlessly, or most ineptly. It was dire, so poor that a man standing next to Karen, Harry and Elliot's mother, asked if he could borrow her copy of *Vogue* (she'd grown tired of this pretence of a game and started reading it after ten minutes). Back then, I was fully committed to the ritual: we would not leave before the bitter end. I now realise I should apologise to Karen for making her endure QPR v Wimbledon. Karen, we should have left early. We should have left at half-time. Sorry (there was no consolation in the result, either. QPR lost the game 1-0).

Nice v PSG wore on. Yet again, John and I had contrived to arrive after Mèfi had done her thing. We didn't even have the sight of an eagle soaring around the Allianz Riviera Stadium to put in our memory bank, to offset this exercise in *ennui*. Ten minutes before the end, I cracked.

'Shall we leave early?' I said.

'Great idea,' said John. 'Let's go.'

The inevitable happened. While we were waiting for the tram to take us back into central Nice, we heard the roar of the crowd. Nice had scored.

'Are you bothered?' I asked.

'I don't care at all,' said John.

Later, I watched video replays showing Neymar lose possession in a stumbling move in Nice's half. Nice swiftly countered. Highly rated young Dutch winger Calvin Stengs sped down the left wing, then crossed for substitute Andy Delort who hit the ball on the half-volley with his right foot. Bang! It smashed off the underside of the crossbar into the net.

Delort scored two minutes from time. It was a stunning goal. The game ended 1-0 to Nice.

When the final whistle sounded, Gouiri flicked the ball up as if he were a freestyle world champion, a foot or two away from Neymar, as if to say: who do you think you are? Neymar gave him a shove for his cheek.

All of this played out right in front of where John and I had been standing. Like John, though, I don't regret leaving when we did. I'm just all the more convinced that the Allianz Riviera stadium is jinxed.

* * *

AS Monaco had to win. It was as simple as that. Failure meant *la chute* – exit from the Europa League. *Nice-Matin* previewed the game with what I couldn't help but think was a more Sartrean headline than you'd find in the UK football press:

'*L'exploit, ou le vide.*' 'Win, or the void.'

Sartre's *Being and Nothingness* had a lot to answer for, but both the existentialist philosopher and pretty much all of the game were off the menu for Monaco's tie against Portugal's Sporting Club de Braga (usually known just as Braga) early evening on Thursday, 17 March. Monaco had lost 2-0 away to Braga in the first leg of this round of 16 Europa League clash and Philippe Clement, appointed as Monaco's new coach on 3 January, had his work cut out. Clement had played 38 times for the Belgian national team, and despite a short spell with Coventry City he spent most of his playing days with Belgium's Club Brugge, whom he'd just taken to two successive league titles. If anyone could rouse Monaco to a win, it was Clement.

For the first and only time of this season on the Med, I decided to watch a game in a bar instead of attend a stadium. The chosen bar was the Ship & Castle in Monaco. I was in good company, with John as well as Monaco fans

Doumé and his brother Nico. There were plenty of TV screens showing the game and Doumé, ever the optimist, confidently predicted a convincing Monaco win.

Monaco fell behind to an Abel Ruiz goal on 20 minutes, but by then I'd already given up trying to watch the game. It was St Patrick's Day. The Ship & Castle may have had enough TV screens, but it had been overrun by the emerald-green local Irish diaspora. I don't know what the official term is – perhaps it's a shamrock hat, or maybe it's a leprechaun hat – but everyone, save for the quartet from Menton, was wearing one. They bobbed in front of each TV screen as often as the barman would pour a pint of Guinness. It was impossible to concentrate. Soon enough, a well-spoken green-clad woman, sitting to my left and not drinking water, started chatting away as if we were long-lost friends.

'Are you from Ireland?'

'No, I'm from Menton.'

'You don't sound like you're from Menton!'

'That's because I'm English.'

'So you're not French?'

'No. I'm not.'

'And you're not Irish?'

'That's right.'

'But you live in Menton.'

'*Exactement.*'

By now, I'd realised she was French.

'I am French and I live here. And I love the Irish!' she declared, blonde hair poking out from underneath a too-large green hat.

'Yes, me too,' I said.

'Why are you here?' she asked.

'I came with my friends to watch the football.'

'What football?'

Before I could reply, she was off, telling me a convoluted story about London, and Monaco, and how she loved Europe, and hated Russia, but not the Russians, because even though Russia had invaded Ukraine there were lots of very nice Russians, and for that reason she wasn't sure about sanctions, I mean, yes, something has to be done, but the sanctions could hurt ordinary people, couldn't they?

When she referred to 'ordinary people', I wasn't sure what she meant. Ordinary Russian billionaires, whose Monaco yachts might have been seized?

I didn't get her name. We had a long conversation, though, during which Monaco looked dangerous but failed to score until the 90th minute, when Axel Diasi levelled the tie. At least, I know Diasi got a goal and I think Monaco looked dangerous – there was too much noise and commotion in the pub to be sure. Anyway, Doumé's and Nico's faces told me all I needed to know. A 1-1 home draw made for a 3-1 defeat on aggregate. It was *la chute* for their team. Or if we're being Sartrean, *le vide*. Nothingness.

Afterwards Clement told Edward Stratmann of the *Monaco-Tribune*, 'I am very disappointed like everyone else, the staff, the players, the managers, the supporters … There are two solutions: you can lower your head, or raise it and bounce back! There are ten league "finals" left until the end of the season. We will have to do our best to win as many as possible and not linger on the disappointment of our elimination. Everything is still possible, but we have to react. I have a lot of young players in this squad, who are logically very disappointed tonight. We have to stay together and show solidarity to create more chances and score goals.'

Two days later, I was back in Monaco. No pub this time, instead the train from Menton to Monaco and then straight to the Stade Louis II. It was AS Monaco v Paris Saint-Germain – another chance to see Messi and Neymar but also, now back from his suspension, Kylian Mbappé. Could Clement instil enough belief in his players, hot on the heels of their Europa League exit? I didn't think so. PSG might have underperformed against Nice at the Allianz Riviera stadium, but Monaco were six points adrift of fifth-placed Strasbourg and weren't exactly scoring for fun, having failed to find the back of the net in two of their past three matches. Surely, the forward trio of Messi, Neymar and Mbappé would put them to the sword. Sorry – I mean, cast them into *le vide*.

But it'd been a busy week, I'd not had a chance to read about the fixture, and when I did, on my phone on the train, I discovered that Messi was not in the starting XI. Apparently, he'd come down with a bout of flu. Would there be no end to his physical travails in Paris? His absence meant he'd now missed 11 games owing to a combination of injuries and illness. He'd appeared a grand total of 26 times across all competitions for PSG, scoring seven goals and chalking up 11 assists.

This was not normal for the seven-time Ballon d'Or winner. He'd barely ever not started for Barcelona.

It got worse. I read that during the previous weekend's 3-0 home win over Bordeaux, PSG's fans had booed

Messi. Not once or twice, but every time he touched the ball. They'd had a go at Neymar as well, but although he too is a star, the booing of Messi was more significant. It was seismic. Here was the world's greatest-ever footballer, greeted by swarms of adoring PSG fans just a few months ago, being treated with contempt. No matter that he'd scored a record-breaking 672 goals in 778 games for Barça. No matter that he'd won 35 trophies in 16 seasons. No matter that it was no small thing to leave Barça; that he could have gone to any club he'd chosen; that he'd chosen to sign for PSG, purchased by Qatar Sports Investments (QSI) in 2011. No matter that PSG were 15 points ahead of second-placed Nice, and guaranteed another Ligue 1 title. The boos and whistles were incessant.

In the wake of his star player having experienced hostility wholly unprecedented in his career, PSG's manager, Mauricio Pochettino, gave a measured comment to the press. He said the players had reacted to the hostility 'with sadness', adding:

'No one who loves PSG, its colours, and who feels the frustration of elimination, can experience it in any other way.

'Sadness. I think that's the right word. The sadness of experiencing an afternoon like this here at the Parc des Princes.

'Messi and Neymar? We are all affected, we understand the disappointment and frustration, which we also share. But we are responsible. We only have to accept it as a team and we will be united until the end.'

PSG fans were furious at the preceding Champions League elimination by Real Madrid. But to boo a player of Messi's calibre? Something deeper must have been at play. I wanted to air my own theory to John – we were attending this game for a *Footy on the Med* podcast – but it was his birthday, I'd treated him to the ticket, and it was perhaps too leaden a topic. But my theory – well, better call it an undeveloped idea – harked back to what I'd found out about Espanyol's club culture. Recall Quim Torrecillas, the lawyer and Espanyol devotee from Blanes on the Costa Brava:

'In Catalunya, we have to support Espanyol. To be a Barça fan is very easy. To follow Espanyol is to be the little shop owner, the small businessman ... the person who doesn't want to have it all and only wants what he truly deserves from the effort he makes in his everyday life. This is what identifies Espanyol and also the way Catalans are. It's really *"La força d'un sentiment"* ("The strength of a feeling").'

I'd always been happy being a Queens Park Rangers fan. I love the way the club plays football. On the deck. Neat. Quick. Tidy. Beautiful, when it's good. A silky number ten, ideally. I love the boxed-in ground, the passion, the energy. I like the family feel to Loftus Road, I like the way the club did the right thing and renamed it the Kiyan Prince Foundation Stadium and, at the time of the Monaco v PSG game, I loved the fact there was a move to rename one of the stands and call it 'The Stanley Bowles Stand'.

I didn't like the Ecclestone and Briatore era. I wasn't bothered if Naomi Campbell was in the ground, I didn't care if the corporate restaurant served Michelin-starred food and, however easy on the eye they were, I could do without the Campbell and Kate Moss lookalikes who were there to meet and greet.

And while I'd been as euphoric as everyone else at Wembley on 24 May 2014, when a Bobby Zamora goal sent the Rs back to the Premier League, I'd had my fill of Premier League dreams. What was the point? Unless the likes of QSI bought the club and committed billions in investment, we wouldn't be able to compete and would hurtle straight back down to the Championship. And if a QSI came along, then what? What was QPR then?

This problem is endemic in modern football. I have no solutions. But I bet, if I went to the bars of Paris and talked to PSG's ultras, they'd probably say Messi is OK really, so is Neymar, and we're sorry we took it out on them, it was out of order, but we were just very frustrated, and not even with the Real Madrid defeat, no, not really, what we hate and can't stand and don't know how much longer we can take is the loss of our identity. You see, Paris Saint-Germain is not Paris Saint-Germain anymore. It's an asset in a portfolio.

* * *

Our seats for AS Monaco v Paris Saint-Germain were in Honneur B2, on the other side of the pitch to those for the Marseille and Real Sociedad games. The visit of such prestigious opponents made the game a near sell-out. The official attendance was 16,642, a couple of thousand under the stadium's 18,523 capacity, and, at €125 a ticket, this was the most expensive game yet on the Med. Seats 50 and 51 in row ten of Honneur B2 didn't deliver value for money size-wise – we were hemmed in like sardines – but they did offer a view of the sea. There it was, away to the west. Perhaps, after all, the Stade Louis II was the closest stadium to the sea.

It would make sense if it was. Work on the stadium finished towards the close of 1984, on land reclaimed from the sea 15 years earlier. The original Stade Louis II, named after Louis II, Prince of Monaco (1870–1949) and opened in 1939, was destroyed to make way for the successor of the same name, an altogether more avant garde proposition with nine huge Olympic arches dominating the western, uncovered away end and a weirdly futuristic terracotta roof over all the other stands. It was the brainchild of architect Henry Pottier (better known for his work on one of the rare high-rise districts in Paris, the Front de Seine to the south of the Eiffel Tower), and it's a marvel of design and engineering, accommodating not just Monaco's football team but also an athletics track and, underneath, a host of facilities including a sports centre, a swimming pool complete with an Olympic diving pool, three levels of car parking, offices and the International University of Monaco.

The new, all bells and whistles Stade Louis II was officially opened by Prince Rainier III on 25 January 1985. The following day, AS Monaco hosted RC Lens. They won 3-0. It was a flying start for the new stadium, which suffered a small technical hiccup: the scoreboard read '30-0'.

How many goals would we see today? Messi was absent, so too Di María. But Kylian Mbappé was back, and on form with 16 goals to date. Neymar was Neymar, a world-class goalscorer. Monaco's star striker, Wissam Ben

Yedder, was also having a fine season with 15 goals to date. Monaco had the most wins against PSG of all Ligue 1's clubs (43 from 91), but they'd only won one of their past five league matches. It was a tough game to call. Probably a 1-1 draw, I reckoned.

After ten minutes, I felt differently. PSG weren't at the races. They looked as if they were playing in second gear. Every now and then Mbappé or Neymar would show a flash of skill. When they did, the effect was as instantaneous as it was evanescent. For a few seconds, it would look as if their team-mates might heft themselves up a gear. Then they'd settle back into second, preferring a lethargic Sunday lunchtime stroll to anything so untoward as exertion.

On 25 minutes, Monaco capitalised thanks to nimble movement by Ben Yedder, who beat Presnel Kimpembe to a near-post cross from Youssouf Fofana and ingeniously flicked the ball into the top corner of the net. It was a fine goal, the kind he could tell his grandchildren about and, unlike Billy Aitken and his seal dribble, there'd be all manner of digital evidence to confirm that *Papi* wasn't away with the fairies. Twitter, YouTube, Instagram – and Ben Yedder, from Sarcelles in Paris, was good friends with Riyad Mahrez, who is from the same place. Who knows, *Papi* might even preserve a congratulatory WhatsApp message from the Manchester City winger and captain of the Algerian national side.

The first half ended with the hosts 1-0 ahead, a Neymar effort curling wide having been PSG's only moment of note. The second half continued in the same vein. PSG looked tired, listless and unimaginative. Mbappé tried a couple of times to rouse himself and his team, to no avail. Substitute Kevin Volland put Monaco 2-0 up in the 68th minute with an adroit, close-range finish, and was then instrumental in Monaco's third goal when he was tripped by Kimpembe. Penalty. No arguments, and Ben Yedder smashed the ball home.

By then, Neymar's temper was getting the better of him. Pochettino took him off, but neither his replacement, Julian Draxler, nor Mauro Icardi (on for Leandro Paredes), made any difference. *Les Monégasques* ran out as thoroughly deserved 3-0 winners.

It was PSG's fourth consecutive away defeat in all competitions. Pochettino did not mince his words.

'The way we lost is not acceptable at this level of competition,' he said. 'We can't start a game the way we started this one.'

Mbappé was more generous. 'They played well, congratulations to them. They're a good team, a great club,' he said. Having won the Ligue 1 title as a Monaco player in 2017, Mbappé was bound to be magnanimous.

After the game, John and I lingered on the walkaway at the top of Honneur B. It's a lofty spot. Far below us were the roads of the Fontvielle quartier, with people scurrying away from the Stade Louis II, past a garage selling Aston Martins and Lamborghinis. High above was Tête de Chien, a 1,804ft rock promontory near the village of La Turbie. A few weeks earlier, Caroline, Maud and I had lunch there in our favourite restaurant on the Riviera, La Fourchette Libre. We'd done what every visitor to La Turbie does and wandered around the remains of the Trophy of Augustus, a 6BC monument built of stone from a nearby quarry to commemorate the Emperor Augustus. Or, specifically, Augustus's victory over the 45 tribes who populated the Alps.

Hats off to Philippe Clement. He'd galvanised his players to a famous victory, too.

* * *

It seems someone at the Stadio Comunale in Sanremo has a literary bent. Inside the stadium is the legend:

'Abandon hope all ye who enter here.'

It's from Dante Alighieri's *Inferno*. It's rendered in English, not Italian.

Whoever decided to harness Dante in the Sanremese cause was either an optimist or a humorist. Despite the imposing archway giving access to the car park beside the ground, despite the menacing stone eagle atop the southern stand, and despite the club's fearsome ultras, the Stadio Comunale is not Europe's most intimidating football ground. It's a homely place where, to judge from their rapport, the fans and players know each other and have a few beers in the same bars after a game.

Arriving there on the afternoon of Wednesday, 30 March for a game due to start at 2.30pm, I doubted Sanremese's opponents had abandoned all hope in their changing room. But they had a job on their hands, nevertheless. Sanremese's fine form had continued and they lay in second place in Serie D, Girone A. Piedmont-based Novara were a few points ahead but a win would have the Italian Riviera club snapping at their heels. Only the first-placed club in each of Serie D's nine regional divisions would be promoted to Serie C, where they could call themselves professional footballers: Serie D, also known as Lega Nazionale Dilettanti, is an amateur league. There was even hope if they finished runners-up. In recent years, many Italian Serie D clubs have failed to meet the financial or regulatory requirements for life in the third tier of Italian football. If the first-placed club fails in this way, the second-placed club replaces them. There is also a play-off among the teams from second to fifth place. Success does not guarantee promotion, but the winner of the play-offs goes on to a list from which the administrators of Serie C may decide to fill a vacancy.

At the other end of the table, there is also a play-off system. The bottom two clubs are automatically relegated to the *Eccellenza*, a regional amateur league, while those from 15th to 18th place battle it out via the play-offs. In addition there is a play-off among the winners of each Girone to decide who gets the bragging rights to the *Scudetto Dilettanti* (the amateur champions' title).

All of this I learned via my phone while waiting for the game to begin. The Italian football league pyramid seemed impossibly chaotic and complicated. Worse, having just finished reading Joe McGinniss's *The Miracle of Castel di Sangro*, it seemed it wasn't exactly unblemished by corruption. Rather as had happened to McGinniss, the story of the miracle, or miracles, left me both heartened and saddened. The first miracle was that which propelled tiny Castel di Sangro Cep 1953 to the dizzy heights of Serie B in 1996. The Abruzzo town only has 6,000 inhabitants, and its football club had spent most of its history in the resolutely amateur *Terza Categoria*. By 1989, Castel di Sangro had achieved promotion to Serie 2, itself a remarkable feat for such a tiny club. Under often obtuse and yet canny manager Osvaldo Jaconi, somehow instead of tumbling out of Serie C and back to amateur status – as many expected – Castel di Sangro hauled themselves into Serie B via a play-off final win against Ascoli. The heroics by goalkeeper Pietro Spinosa, who hadn't played all season, were all the more remarkable given that Jaconi brought him on purely for the penalty shoot-out.

McGinniss was captivated from afar. He left his home in the United States to install himself in Castel di Sangro and chronicle their efforts to avoid relegation in their second year in Serie B. This, their second miracle, they achieved, and McGinniss brilliantly captures the camaraderie, spirit and humility of the players, at the same time as not pulling his punches when it came to the sinister owner, Pietro Rezza, and his henchman-in-chief, Gabriele Gravina, Castel di Sangro's chief of operations.

The Miracle of Castel di Sangro has another miracle, too: McGinniss's conversion to *calcio*. He lives, eats and sleeps football as much as Jaconi and his players. From not speaking a word of Italian, by the end of the season he's learned the language. A man in his 50s, he is childlike in his enthusiasm and lust for life as it's lived in Castel di Sangro and by all those connected with its football club.

But embedded though he was, McGinniss never forsook his fidelity to the book he's writing. He would only write the truth.

So when, at the end of season, McGinniss overhears a group of Castel players talking about how their final game – away to Bari – will pan out, he listens. He listens intently. He knows that Castel di Sangro are already safe from relegation. He knows that Bari need a win to be assured of promotion to Serie A. And he can't believe his ears. The fix is in. Castel di Sangro's players will roll over, have their tummies tickled and concede three goals. For their biddability, they'll be allowed to score a consolation goal via a penalty.

Which is exactly what happened. Bari 3 Castel di Sangro 1. Bari are up. Job well done by the fixers.

McGinniss is horrified. He tells everyone what he thinks. The players urge him to forget about what he heard. They ask him not to put it in his book. One of them reminds him that Italy is the land of Machiavelli as well as Dante. His time in Castel di Sangro is forever jaundiced, the gentle miracle of McGinniss's own immersion in *calcio* has taken a hammering. I'd put down the book in admiration at McGinniss's courage but upset that he'd experienced so unwholesome an epiphany. Friendships that could and should have endured for life, across continents, were surely forever sullied. As he put it in the epilogue, 'And don't we all wish it had ended differently.'

Fresh from the book in the Stadio Comunale, my libel lawyer's mind wondered about the conversations between publishers and author once McGinniss had delivered the manuscript. Many publishers would not risk publishing a book so clearly defamatory as *The Miracle of Castel di Sangro*. Those that did would want to know they had a cast-iron defence of truth. McGinniss must have convinced his publishers. *The Miracle* had been in print for more than 20 years now, although Gravina had filed criminal charges against McGinniss in Italy before he'd finished the book. McGinniss faced a potential 12-year prison sentence but the Ministry of Justice in Rome threw out Gravina's claim. Gravina did not mind. Initially, he told the press, 'McGinniss likes Italy. Let's see how much he likes Italian justice.' When the charges were dismissed, he said he wasn't surprised, adding, 'In any event, my only reason for bringing these charges was to block publication of his book in Italy, and in this I have succeeded.'

McGinniss had the last laugh. Radical-left publisher Kaos Edizioni took on the book, publishing it in Italy on 9 April 2001. Still later, a 2018 documentary on Italian TV channel La7 confirmed the Bari game had been fixed, thanks to testimony from some of the very Castel di Sangro players McGinniss knew. By then, the New York-born author was dead. He died in Worcester, Massachusetts on 10 March 2014 of pneumonia and septic shock secondary to metastatic prostate cancer.

What would McGinniss have made of Gravina's rise to eminence? The law graduate and former Castel di Sangro Cep 1953 president is not merely an honorary citizen of Castel di Sangro (this honour was bestowed on him on 14 December 2014). He is the president of the Italian Football Federation, an office he assumed on 22 October 2018. As of 20 April 2021, when 53 of 55 possible votes went in his favour, Gravina is also a member of the UEFA executive committee.

As we arrived, a banner was unfurled and draped over the railings of the lower Gradinata Nord stand. On it, in blue and white stencilled capital letters against a white background, were the words 'LA SANREMESE E LA MIA SQUADRA DEL CUORE'. I think this means 'Sanremese – My Heart, My Team'. Sanremese's loyal supporters were filing into the stand, blue and white scarves around their necks, one or two with blue and white flags on poles, eager to start waving them in honour of the team about to take to the pitch. If games really are fixed regularly in Italy, what do the *tifosi* make of this? Is it just a fact of life? 'Politics have no relation to morals,' said Machiavelli. Was that it? For politics looms large in football, of that there can be no doubt. Or is it different now? Has Italian football moved away from the dark days where brown envelopes would change hands and secure the fate of the football club? Or maybe *grande Joe* got it wrong. Rezza and Gravina were just a pair of good old boys who did what they had to do and *pretended* to order their players to throw the Bari game, when of course the fix was never in, because they wanted them to take it easy and avoid injuries in this, the final game of an incredible season, so that next year, why, there would even be another miracle – promotion to Serie A!

The referee blew his whistle. I'd started to tell John about *The Miracle of Castel di Sangro*, but it was time to watch the game. Asti, in 15th place, needed a win or at least a draw. Sanremese had to keep pushing at Novara. Both sets of players did not hold back. Hard tackle followed hard tackle, but Sanremese were the better side. Their number ten, Giorgio Gagliardi, was tricky, quick-thinking and clever. Emanuele Anastasia, wearing the number seven shirt, looked dangerous on the wing. And there, in goal, was the young man John and I had so warmed to, Jacopo Malaguti from Bologna. We fancied he looked a bit older. Of course, he would do, but we thought he'd gained a couple of years rather than a few months. We realised he'd grown a beard. 'It does make him look older,' said John. 'He looks at least 15 now.'

The youthful Malaguti performed as confidently as ever, which was just as well because Sanremese contrived to turn dominance into difficulty when Daniel Gemignani took the knees away from an Asti player so viciously that he was given a straight red card. It was one of the most bizarre cameos I've ever seen: Gemignani had come on as 26th-minute substitute, and only lasted 14 minutes before he was sent off, for a challenge he didn't need to make. The Asti player was in his own half.

Asti's half-time team talk had the desired effect. They were raring to go and began to exploit their man advantage. Soon, they were ahead. Alessio Ciletta got on the score sheet but only thanks to an uncharacteristic mistake by Malaguti. Ciletta hoisted in a hopeful cross from the left wing, but no Asti players were anywhere near Malaguti, who watched the ball all the way and yet inexplicably managed to paw it into his own net. The poor lad was distraught. How he must have loathed the fine saves his opposite number then started making, denying Gagliardi with a spectacular diving stop to his left. No goalkeeper's union this afternoon; all Malaguti prayed for was for his team-mates to score an equaliser and, if the Asti keeper Silvio Brustolin happened to be at fault for a goal, so be it. Gagliardi nearly got one with a left-footed shot that cannoned off the bar, but then came Sanremese's moment. Substitute Filippo Scalzi was fouled as he cut into the box from the right: penalty. Emmanuele Anastasia slotted it home with ease.

Sanremese might have gone on to win the match, but Brustolin was having one of those games. He made save after save, Sanremese hit the post, Asti hit the crossbar and then, when all was said, done, savagely kicked and roughly tackled, it ended as a 1-1 draw.

John and I were delighted. We'd grown to like Sanremese, and we loved Malaguti.

As for the young goalkeeper, every single one of his team-mates clustered around him at the end, to embrace him, pat him on the back, ruffle his hair and tell him it was all OK.

I imagine some games in Italy are still fixed but this one wasn't. Each player on the pitch at the Stadio Comunale was as honest as the day is long.

11

April 2022

Also a Normal One

JOHN WAS his usual bubbly self when we met at Menton-Garavan train station on Sunday, 3 April. We were heading to Genoa again, this time for the visit of José Mourinho's AS Roma, who were in town to take on Sampdoria. It would be a tough game for the hosts. They didn't look like relegation fodder, mainly because the clubs beneath them were so poor, but 16th position in the 20-team Serie A table wasn't a place of comfort. Roberto D'Aversa had paid the price for *La Samp*'s stuttering form, dismissed in January after just a few months in charge, and the club had turned to former manager Marco Giampaolo. Unfortunately for him, the *Blucerchiati* continued to lurch between triumph and defeat. They'd overcome Venezia 2-0 at the Stadio Pier Luigi Penzo in their most recent game, but had lost four and won one of the previous five matches.

In contrast, Mourinho had Roma purring. Life at Spurs might not have worked out for him – sacked after

17 months in April 2021, this was the first time Mourinho had left a club without winning any silverware since 2002 – but he'd got off to a flying start with Roma, whom he joined on 4 May, and hadn't looked back. Italy's three-time domestic league champions (and nine-time Coppa Italia winners) were pushing for Europe, English striker Tammy Abraham, who'd signed for Roma in August 2021 from Chelsea, was scoring a goal every other game, and the club had just brushed Lazio aside in a 3-0 win in the *Derby della Capitale.* There were a currently seventh, and a win would nudge Roma into the top six.

Associazione Sportiva Roma, founded on 7 June 1927, is a club with many nicknames. They include *I Giallorossi* (The Yellow and Reds); *La Lupa* (The She-Wolf); *La Magica* (The Magic One); *Capitolini* (Capitoline); *Lupetti* (Little Cubs); and *Lupi* (Wolves). Their crest features a she-wolf set against a golden yellow background. Below, half of the crest is in carmine red, with the legend 'ROMA – 1927'. Just straddling the red section, mainly set against the deep yellow of the upper half, are two infants: Romulus and Remus, the founders of Rome. The city's mythology has it that they were brought up by a she-wolf; wolves are Rome's sacred animals. The yellow colouring is in homage to the Roman gods, the red to Rome's emperors.

Given Roma's recent form – they were unbeaten in their past nine matches – John and I felt that either *La Lupa* or *Lupi* was the apposite name for the day. We couldn't see *La Samp* being anything other than devoured.

* * *

We knew the drill well by now. Short train ride to Ventimiglia. Wait for half an hour or so. Time enough for a coffee in the station cafe or a beer in the cluster of nearby bars. Board the train to Genova Piazza Principe. If there were no delays, walk the 35 minutes to the Stadio Luigi Ferraris. If there was a delay, hop in a cab. Either way, there'd be time for a pre-match drink and then we were there, in the queue for the Distinti stand. Back at the Stadio Luigi Ferraris. Back at a great stadium that felt like a home from home. Back to soak up the intensity, enjoy the theatre and hope that the chain-smoker had seen the light, thrown all his cigarettes away and was now radiating nothing beyond an aroma of nicotine-free saintliness.

There was one thing we didn't check. The train times back. Or rather, we knew there'd be time to get a train back to Ventimiglia after the game. That felt close enough to Menton not to worry unduly. Still, while we were waiting at Ventimiglia, I tried to check. I was torn between trying to decipher the timetables in the station or looking up the times on my phone. John wasn't worried and chatted away, and I gave up. I'd been going back and forth between Italy and France enough by now to know that its trains operate to their own inner needs, not anything so prosaic as a timetable. Besides, there'd either be a train or there wouldn't. If not, we could get a cab.

There was another reason for not double-checking everything. April was going to be a heavy month. Caroline, Maud and I would be driving back to Cornwall to pack up our house. I had to get to a few work meetings in London and elsewhere. We'd be seeing various members of our families too. Every day we would be doing something, somewhere. No rest for the Brexit escapees. All in, we'd be in the UK for some two weeks, before driving back to Menton again. There'd be precious little football, although I had an eye to trying to have a game with the old Penzance crew.

Whenever I thought about all things ahead, not just in April but in May too (it'd take a good three trips back to the UK to sort out the house ahead of its sale), I felt overwhelmed not just by stress but also by confusion. Had we made the right decision? Hadn't life become just a bit too complicated? What if we'd never come to France and just stayed put in Penzance?

All of this was tumbling around in my mind on the day of Sampdoria v Roma. And the great thing was that I knew, within 20 minutes or so of meeting John, I'd relax, decide to forget about everything and just enjoy a day out watching the footy with a mate. This was exactly how the day went, until the train pulled into Varazze. At this point, with the sea I'd swum in some 40 years ago maybe a couple of hundred yards away, John asked an uncanny question: 'When did you first come to the Med?'

Cue the tale of my parents' road-trip through Europe, meeting Cristina, her coming to stay with me in the UK the following summer, me going to Brumano for three weeks. I told John my time in Brumano had been the happiest three weeks of my life. Again I felt the urge to return. If not now, when? It couldn't be more than a four-or-five-hour drive from Menton. Could I tag on a trip to the end of our return drive from Cornwall? No, too far out of the way. It wouldn't happen in April; we'd be in the

UK too much and it just wasn't practical. But I had to get
there. We only had a few months left of living in France.
If I didn't get to Brumano now I probably never would. It
felt urgent and essential. I wanted to walk onto the football
pitch in the middle of the tiny village, smell the grass and
look at the mountains.

The conversation returned to football. John had been
in goal for much of the last five-a-side game we'd played,
with Doumé and his crew of mainly French lads. Big
though he is, John can leap about in goal with the agility
of a 20-year-old – when he wants to and so long as he's not
hungover. For this particular game, he was nursing a very
sore head. Movement of any kind was beyond him. There
is a five-year age gap between us (in John's favour), but for
once I felt as if I wasn't the most immobile player on the
pitch. Goal after goal flew past the statuesque O'Hare.
It would have been remiss not to bring this up: expats
though we were, the English tradition of taking the mick
out of your friends was alive and well with us. Not only
did John take it, he told me how he'd once been dishing
it out, perhaps a bit too much, when someone shot back
at him, 'Who are you, anyway? You're just a poor man's
Iain Dowie.' With no disrespect to Dowie, John is a good-
looking bloke. This was harsh and I said as much. John
said he'd enjoyed the line a lot: you have to take a good
comeback when one's sent your way. And then he said,
'Did you say one of the lads we played with has a brother
who plays for Sampdoria?'

This was true. For a recent game, a few of Doumé's
usual pool of players were missing, he'd rung round and
two Italian lads had turned up. One was called Mateo.

His brother is Tommaso Augello, a 5ft 11in defender who was born in Milan. Augello had worked his way up from Serie D to Serie C and then, with Spezia, he found himself playing in Serie B. In 2019, Sampdoria signed him on loan. The deal was made permanent in 2020. A quick check on the phone revealed Augello wasn't in the first XI for Roma's visit, but he was a substitute. He was 27 years old.

I'd asked Mateo, a decent player himself, if he was a Sampdoria fan. 'No, Milan,' he laughed. He was proud of his brother, though. You'd have to be. It's hard enough to make it as a professional footballer but to keep going through each division in the Italian football pyramid, and find yourself facing a team managed by José Mourinho! Tommaso Augello didn't lack for a work ethic.

Augello came on, too. In the 60th minute, he replaced Nicola Murru. He went on to have a good game, but by then Roma had gone into cruise control. Leading in the 27th minute thanks to Henrikh Mkhitaryan poking in the ball from very close range, Mourinho had more than enough nous to ensure his players came away with a win. They were slick and well-drilled, taking the sting out of any rare Sampdoria pressure and always looking as if they might add to Mkhitaryan's goal. The English pair, Abraham up front and Chris Smalling in defence, played well (though Abraham snatched at a back-pass gifted to him in the 38th minute, scuffing it well wide with his left foot when he should have scored). *La Samp*'s Antonio Candreva was as technically excellent as ever, but one man can't win a football match. Candreva also failed to beat the first defender with a corner towards the end of the match, and I couldn't help but wonder if I was watching a man age, as if the season and, before that, years of playing in the top flight was just starting to catch up with him. The game ended 1-0 to Roma, who moved up to fifth place. The score flattered Sampdoria.

As ever at the Stadio Luigi Ferraris, it felt as if we'd been part of a carnival. Roma brought a lot of supporters; they couldn't rival the Sampdoria din but they did their best. Throughout, Samp fans waved flags and banners, sang and chanted. At one point, they broke out into a rendition of Boney M's 'Rivers of Babylon'. It was unmistakeable. We'd not heard them sing this before. What was the reason? Was it regularly sung? Was it a new thing?

As he left the pitch, José Mourinho looked content. That's one word. Another is 'normal'. The self-declared 'Special One' had no trace of the half-snarl that so often formed on his face, as if, even when he was happy, something deep inside was making him very unhappy indeed. He wasn't lording it over the home side or their fans. There was no hint of arrogance. He looked like a grey-haired man in his late-50s who'd had a nice walk with the dogs in his local park. He was happy with his lot, happy with life. A normal one, after all.

With the game over by 7.45pm, John and I nipped into the Ristorante Edilio a minute or two from the exit on the north-east corner of Stadio Luigi Ferraris. For an unaccountable reason, I thought it was Michelin-starred. 'It'd be an odd place for a Michelin-starred restaurant,' observed John. It wasn't, and it served mainly seafood. I don't eat fish, but some steak was on the menu too. We whiled away nearly an hour there, before jumping in an

Uber and arriving at Genova Piazza Principe just in time for the train to Ventimiglia.

It had been a great day out. Not the world's best football match, but Roma were a good side. Abraham and Smalling were good. Our mate Mateo's brother was good, when he came on. It's always good to see Candreva play. We hoped Sampdoria would stay up, and that we'd come back to the Stadio Luigi Ferraris soon. We both felt a new-found affection for Mourinho, too. 'Maybe he's a nice guy underneath it all?' mused John.

Then I remembered something a friend connected with QPR had told me. After the horrific Grenfell Tower fire in June 2017, QPR, the football club closest to the site, hosted the Game 4 Grenfell on 2 September 2017. Two teams – Team Ferdinand, managed by QPR icon 'Sir' Lesley Ferdinand, and Team Shearer, managed by Alan Shearer – played a match to raise money for those affected by the fire at Loftus Road. The ground was packed and 17,468 watched as Team Ferdinand won 5-3 on penalties. The game was aired live on Sky 1. Mourinho came on as a sub for David James of Team Shearer. He was booked for time-wasting and had some stern words for his defence when Team Shearer conceded a second goal, making for a 2-2 draw and penalties. If that sounds typically Mourinho, it was very much tongue-in-cheek. My friend told me he'd hammed up his bad guy image. On the day, Mourinho had been courtesy itself to everyone.

For John, this prompted an echo of Roma's most famous player, Francesco Totti. The one-club man *par excellence. L'Ottavo Re di Roma*, as the Romans say – 'the eighth king of Rome'. Totti spent his entire career at

Roma, winning the Serie A title once, two Coppa Italias, two Supercoppa Italianas, and, in scoring 250 goals (in 619 appearances), becoming the second-highest scorer of all time in Italian league history (the top scorer is Silvio Piola who netted 290 league goals in his career). Oh, and Totti also won the 2006 World Cup and was UEFA Euro 2000 finalist with Italy.

'I was in Rome the day he announced his retirement,' said John. 'The whole place fell silent. It was as if the Pope had died.'

Football elevates its heroes, but, because we watch them week in, week out, we feel we know them. Their actions touch us like a member of the family. Totti, the legend, was retiring: the whole of Rome was in shock. Mourinho, the master of mind-games, was actually an affable, charming man.

A great day, we agreed, as the train rolled into Ventimiglia.

Needless to say, there was no connecting train to Menton. It was 11.30pm. There were no taxis. Only one hotel was open. The proprietor said it was full. We couldn't even sleep in his storeroom. We asked the police by the station what we should do. They shrugged their shoulders. There were a lot of them, idling in cars and vans, on the look-out for migrants (who, if they make it past the Ventimiglia police and on to a train to France, are often hauled off the train at Menton-Garavan by the French police).

We set off to walk. It was raining. It would take us at least two hours. I didn't like the idea of walking two hours in the cold and the rain. I went back to the police and remonstrated. Were we really supposed to walk back to Menton? On a night like this? Any chance of a lift?

Italian justice looked favourably on my pleas. A police officer in plain clothes, who'd appeared out of the shadows in an unmarked car, told his colleague in the passenger seat to make a call. It was to a friend of theirs who was a taxi driver. He clambered out of bed, put some clothes on, came down to the station and drove us home over the border to Menton.

12

May 2022

Buona Fortuna

APRIL WASN'T the cruellest month, but it was as busy as I'd expected. A lot of it was spent in southern England before the long drive from Calais down to Menton. Before I knew it, in early May, I was back in Cornwall again. This time, I was on my own, to continue packing and be around for the removal men taking the first of what would be two loads of our things into storage. Why storage? The house we'd found in Wiltshire was a probate sale. There was some complexity to the estate and we were told there were significant post-Covid delays anyway when it came to obtaining a grant of probate. With luck, we'd be able to move in by the end of August, in time for Maud to start in a new Wiltshire school in September. But our buyers had a buyer, everyone was eager to get on with things and we didn't feel we could make people wait indefinitely. Putting everything into storage seemed the right thing to do.

Being back in Cornwall, alone, was bittersweet. I saw my sons. I had a game or two with the five-a-side crew I'd played with for years. I saw dear, close friends. I checked in with the neighbours. The life I'd lived in Cornwall had been a good one. It was all still there. My sons were there.

Another wobble. Maybe we could just call the whole thing off? Come home from France to Penzance? Pick up where we'd left everything?

I knew we couldn't. Caroline needed to be near her family. I had a new job that would require a lot of meetings in London. Post-Covid, there was a discernible shift in the professional sector, a sense that the endless Zoom, Teams, Chime or whatever calls of the pandemic had been fine then, but now it was time to re-embrace the office, the water-cooler chat, the canteen and, yes, the commute. Penzance was too far away. Wiltshire ticked all the boxes. Not too far from London, and not too far from East Devon, Bristol and Cornwall, where our families lived. Once we were living in Wiltshire, it'd be breeze to get to London for work or to nip down to Cornwall to see Harry and Elliot (and, if they'd still have me, get a game in with the lads).

In Cornwall, I packed and cleaned and sorted. My books were a day's work alone. There are too many of them. Worse, still, are my newspaper and magazine cuttings. There are hundreds upon hundreds, yellowing and dusty and torn, in tired cardboard boxes. Why I keep them I don't know. I will never, in my dotage, plough through them and put all the cuttings in chronological order in neat ring-binders, for no one ever to read but for someone to shove in their attic and say, 'We really should get rid of Dad's cuttings,' only to feel bad, gently curse and leave them where they are. One of the boxes was so battered it disintegrated as soon as I moved it. Out fell some stories I'd written for the nationals many years ago.

I flicked through them. There was a piece from April 2002 about climbing Mount Elbrus in Russia. Another one on interviewing the head of a law firm. The supervening time had vanished but clichés are evergreen. I know this because, on a whim, I rifled around in search of stories written in April. I'd often keep not just a cut-out of one of my pieces, but the section in which it had appeared. 'April is the cruellest month' was rolled out in headings or standfirsts with the regularity of a metronome, a deadened shorthand that bears no resemblance to its original meaning. This I only remembered when I came across a volume of Eliot's collected poetry. I looked up one of my favourite poems, *'La Figlia Che Piange'* [The Crying Daughter]. During the year of my pen-pal relationship with Cristina, I'd read it again and again. I think I even sent letters to her in which I copied the line 'Weave, weave the sunlight in your hair'. Of course, I hadn't understood the poem. I'd been carried away by its sound. Eliot's narrator wasn't looking for love, he was looking for a monument to a literary conceit. The woman in *La Figlia* is a plaything of his imagination. There's no mention of her hair colour, either.

All the years of trotting out that yes, *'La Figlia Che Piange'* is my favourite Eliot poem.

Granted, it wasn't something that came up often. Neither John nor, for that matter, any of my friends had ever asked me which Eliot poem had most moved me. But for the first time in a long time, I sat down. To be still. To do nothing. To think. What else had I misunderstood? I turned to *The Wasteland*. There was that famous line, and its less popularised successors:

April is the cruellest month, breeding
Lilacs out of the dead land, mixing
Memory and desire, stirring
Dull roots with spring rain.

Eliot wrote *The Wasteland* after the influenza pandemic of 1918 to 1819, which killed millions of people worldwide. His wasteland is a place we all feared might happen, when Covid began. For Eliot, who'd had what was then described as 'the Spanish flu', April is the cruellest month because, for those still living in the post-pandemic wasteland, it's just a memory. It kindles hope, only to spit in its face.

It was a relief to be back in France, back home with Caroline and Maud. Within days, we were off again to the easternmost tip of the Italian Riviera – La Spezia. The gateway to the world-famous Cinque Terre, La Spezia draws tourists from all over the world, all year round. The Cinque Terre is very pretty and lovely. No one could possibly knock the five villages of Monterosso al Mare, Vernazza, Corniglia, Manarola, and Riomaggiore. There are no cars. The villages cling to the cliffs overlooking the Ligurian sea. People potter along the paths linking the villages or take the train. They stop to rest and swim and eat. Then they leave, revived by their step back in time.

But I'd also say, if you like football and want to see a game with a pumping atmosphere in a jaw-dropping setting, go to La Spezia. Go there as soon as you can. For La Spezia's football club, Spezia Calcio, are a gem of Italian football.

* * *

I knew little about Spezia Calcio before the trip. What I did know was that I'd have covered the length of Riviera football in Italy and France if I saw a game at the club's small, exposed and, for the visit of Atalanta at least, electrifying stadium. Thanks to Caroline and Helén, who took the kids and dogs to the Cinque Terre for the day, John and I not only had an afternoon's football ahead of us, but there was also time for a drink in the Dal Toscana 1890 bar on the way to the Stadio Alberto Picco. The bar verged on rough with a fair number of rowdy, semi-inebriated local fans, and John went inside to get a second round. He disappeared long enough for me to find out more about Spezia Calcio.

This was Spezia's second season in Serie A. Their manager was Thiago Motta, capped 30 times by Italy and formerly of Barcelona, Atlético Madrid, Genoa, Inter Milan and Paris Saint-Germain. Motta won 27 major titles with all his clubs combined. Brazilian by birth, he was capped twice by Brazil before acquiring Italian citizenship, and had been appointed as Spezia Calcio's boss on 5 July 2021. He was much admired in Spezia, having kept one of the division's smallest clubs in Serie A by the end of his first season. But could he do it again? Spezia's first half of the season had been poor. They'd spent all their time hovering around the relegation zone. But today, they were 16th. They'd won 17 points in the second half of the season, which made for one more than in the first half with three games yet to play. A full seven points clear of the drop zone, they seemed set to survive their second successive Serie A season. Set to survive, yes, but a win against Atalanta would go a long way to calming Spezian nerves.

But Motta, a combative defensive midfielder as a player, was not eyeing an easy fixture. Atalanta, based in Bergamo in northern Italy, finished third in Serie A the previous season, earning their fourth successive Champions League qualification. Founded in 1907, Atalanta were a solid, respectable club, with 61 seasons in Serie A, 28 in Serie B and only one in Serie C. They'd won the Coppa Italia once and Serie B six times. As a Serie B club, they'd managed to reach the semi-finals of the European Cup Winners' Cup in the 1987/88 season. They lost to the eventual surprise winners, Belgian club Mechelen, but this achievement – getting to the semi-final of a major UEFA competition as a club outside the top division – has been matched only by Cardiff City. All in all, the black and blue vertical stripes of Atalanta, or *I Nerazzurri*, could boast a far heftier record than Spezia Calcio. Even Spezia's solitary crowning as Divisione Nazionale victors was not quite the clean sweep of a typical league title. Set against the backdrop of wartime, in 1944 the Italian Football Federation split the teams into regional groups, leading to play-offs and eventually a finals stage. Spezia prevailed over Venezia and Torino.

Now, on a cloudless and hot day in early May, Atalanta needed a win to keep their European dreams alive, even if, sitting in eighth place, those dreams could almost certainly ascend no higher than Europa Conference League football. The game pitted *I Bianchi* (The Whites) or *Aquile* (The Eagles) at home to perhaps Italian football's most agreeably nicknamed club, *La Dea* (The Goddess).

How nice to have been christened with the name Atalanta, the Greek goddess of running, resulting in fans imploring their goddess to triumph. And how good of the Premier League's Eagles to donate a second-hand kit to the Swiss banker Hermann Hurri, who founded Spezia in 1906. Hurri played for Crystal Palace and was given a turn-of-the-century Palace kit, of light blue and white. Spezia's players turned out in it for a few years, before opting for the kit they still play in today – white shirts, black shorts and black socks.

Both sides had enough to play for: this wasn't a meaningless end-of-season run-out. Both had patchy form going into the match. It was a difficult game to call. I was just about to look up the odds when John returned. Only then did I realise he'd been gone for ten, maybe 15, minutes.

'She tried to short-change me!' he said, aghast.

'No! Are you sure?'

'Sure as sure can be. I gave her €20 and she tried to give me change for ten.'

'Was that why you were so long?'

'Mainly, yes. She didn't understand what I was saying.'

'But eventually you made yourself understood?'

'I think so. She gave the change for a 20, anyway.'

The Stadio Alberto Picco was a good ten-minute walk away. At this rate, we'd miss the kick-off. A noisy bunch of early-20s men on the table next to ours was getting noisier. The one nearest to me had heard English being spoken. He'd started to lean in a little in our direction. Perhaps he'd understood what we'd been talking about. Perhaps this was his favourite bar. Perhaps he was simmering with outrage at this affront to the integrity of the bar staff. Perhaps the woman behind the bar was his wife.

'Come on, let's drink up,' I said. 'I'm sure it was an honest mistake.'

* * *

'Did you see that?! Unbelievable! That was one of the best bits of skill I've ever seen!'

I'd missed it. Sitting in the uncovered north-eastern end of the Stadio Alberto Picco, I'd been distracted by an Italian couple to my left. They were smartly dressed, as many Italians are (though not so much at football matches). They were absorbed in the game, the man especially shouting encouragement and insults every other minute, the woman less vociferous but just as wrapped up in the fortunes of Spezia Calcio. But in a lull they turned to me and, in faltering English, the woman began a conversation.

'Where is you from?'

'I'm from England,' I said.

'Ah, then why is you here?'

'I love football,' I said.

'You like the Spezia?'

'Yes, very much so! I love Spezia. This stadium is fantastic.'

'Good, good, very good,' they said. 'We thought you are from Genoa. We don't like Genoa.'

'No, I'm not from Genoa. Are they your biggest rivals?'

I'm not sure they understood the question perfectly, but they got the gist.

'Yes, they are. We hate Genoa.'

I wondered if we should try speaking in French.

'*Scusa, non parlo Italiano. Parlez-vous Français?*'

Negative. We continued to talk in English.

'You are Spezia fans?' I asked, a statement of the obvious if ever there was one.

'Yes, we love Spezia! We come here all the times.'

'Do you think you will stay up?'

'*Scusa?*'

I took a few more attempts but then they understood.

'*Si! Si*! But we has must to win today if we can.'

'I hope you win and stay up,' I said. '*Buona fortuna!*'

It was just then that John saw a Spezia player control the ball on his chest with his back to goal, turn and hit a half-volley from outside the penalty box that was inches wide. No matter. I'd find it online later. There'd already been plenty to savour. *Le Dea*'s first goal was cleverly worked, seasoned Columbian striker Luis Muriel playing a one-two with Ruslan Malinovskyi before beating two players to send a low right-footed shot past Ivan Provedel in the Spezia goal. In the Curva Piscina among the Spezia fans, John and I had a perfect view of what was a textbook move and finish. It was route one for the next goal by Daniele Verde. Giulio Maggiore sent a ball over the top of Atalanta's defensive line, which was so high it was in the Spezia half. Verde, 26 and bubbling under as an Italian international with Under-19, Under-20 and under-21 appearances so far, kept his composure to round Juan Musso, *Le Dea*'s Argentine keeper, and fire the ball home with his left foot. It was Verde's seventh goal of the season. The stadium erupted.

It was 1-1 at half-time, but Spezia were lucky. Playing a 4-4-2 against Atalanta's 3-4-2-1, they were being outplayed everywhere on the pitch. Balls over the top to Verde seemed to be the game plan. We doubted it'd succeed. Muriel was a constant menace and shot a whisker wide of the post on the hour. It was only a matter of time before Atalanta took the lead. Albanian international Berat Djimsiti did the honours some ten minutes later, scoring with a close-range header from a set piece. Still Atalanta pressed. Jérémie Boga hit the bar and although Emmanuel Gyasi should have done better with a rare Spezia chance, which he created with a brilliant piece of control before turning his man, only to shoot wide, there was only one team in it. Atalanta made sure of the win with an 87th-minute goal by Croatian midfielder Mario Pašalić. Again Muriel was involved, teeing the ball up for Pašalić to send a clever side-footed shot low into the bottom-left corner of the net. The goal was Pašalić's fifth goal in the three games against Spezia.

Pašalić would have fond memories of this trip to La Spezia. So would I. The Stadio Alberto Picco is a wonderful little ground. Both ends behind the goals, the Curva Ferrovia and the Curva Piscina, are exposed, while the two stands running the length of the pitch are covered. The stadium can hold 10,336; 9,000 were there for Spezia v Atalanta. They kept up a rumpus for the whole 90 minutes. All around are the lush hills of Liguria, hatched with villas and houses. Across the road is the port, tall ships and centuries of maritime history. A 20-minute walk and you're in the centre of the city. Beyond, there's the Cinque Terre, and there, at La Spezia's railway station, were Caroline and Helén and our children and the dogs, fresh from a day spent at Levanto, slightly beyond the

Cinque Terre but the nearest dog-friendly beach. Everyone was happy. Spezia's boisterous ultras, some of whom had been at the Dal Toscana 1890 bar, were happy – even in defeat. Everyone had moseyed amiably out of the ground, past the naval college and back to their lives, with no aggro or rancour. How could you be anything other than content with your lot if you lived here? The flares and firecrackers and bangers, the swearing and banners and flags, the perpetual chanting and singing and drumming – it was theatre, a pose, a descent into carnival for three or four hours on a given day, the day of a match. Rarely did it lead to actual violence. Maybe the Mediterranean did influence its football clubs and players, after all.

Then again, there was the Nice v Marseille game. The clash of the ultras at Imperia v Sanremo. The two scariest men I'd ever seen at Sanremese's Stadio Comunale. Stories in *Nice-Matin* of insulting songs sung by the Populaire Sud at the Allianz Riviera. They'd mocked Emiliano Sala, who, having just signed for Cardiff City from Nantes, was killed in January 2019 in a plane crash when a Piper Malibu disappeared off Alderney in the English Channel. Nice had just lost the Coupe de France to Nantes. The *capo* who led his comrades in attacks on Sala at Nice's next home game, against Saint-Étienne on Wednesday, 11 May, must have thought this would show some justified contempt for those who embraced *le jeu à la nantaise* (Nice didn't agree; he was banned for life).

Maybe Gianluca, at the Sanremese v Casale game back in October, was right. Football was football. The good, the bad and the ugly all mixed together in one almighty familial mess, sometimes making for beauty.

There was also the man I'd spoken with in the Curva Piscina at the end of the game. He was a Spezia fan and spoke very good English. He was sanguine in defeat. 'We will stay up,' he said. 'It'll be OK.' He asked which players had caught my eye. I plumped for Verde but he was even-handed and wanted to know who I rated in the Atalanta team. 'Muriel and Pašalić,' I told him, and he agreed. He had kind eyes and a kind face. I asked if it was true, do Spezia's fans dislike Genoa?

'We like Sampdoria,' he said. 'We have a good relationship with them. But we hate Genoa. There was an incident recently. We really hate them.'

13

May 2022

The Other Champions

THE STADIUM in Cagnes-sur-Mer named after Pierre Sauvaigo, a French politician and lawyer, is not so much a stadium and more a multi-purpose community sports centre. There are multiple tennis courts, a skate park, a gym and two artificial football pitches. An athletics track circles the main pitch, which is where Cagnes-Le Cros play their matches. The club's website claims the Stade Pierre Sauvaigo can hold 1,500 people, but it's hard to see how. There's just one small, covered stand, facing east. It's bigger than Villefranche SJB's minuscule stretch of terracing, but it's difficult to imagine 1,500 people crammed inside.

I visited the Stade Pierre Sauvaigo on Sunday, 15 May. The Spezia game was my last on the Italian Riviera; Cagnes-Le Cros's 3pm fixture against Carnoux FC would be the final match on the French Riviera. By then, Paris Saint-Germain had long since won Ligue 1. They wrapped it up on 23 April with a 1-1 draw with Lens and four matches to spare – a record-equalling tenth triumph. With joint ten-time title-winners Saint-Étienne looking doomed to Ligue 2 football, PSG's billions would probably secure the outright record of an 11th title in 2023. Meanwhile, Marseille, Monaco, Nice and Rennes continued to jostle for places two to five, while Montpellier had fallen away and languished in the lower mid-table. To my knowledge, Menton had occupied the second from bottom spot in Regional 1 of the Mediterranean league as if it were an excellent place to be, rather than a scene of *la chute*, not budging from it ever since the January game at the Stade Lucien Rhein. Cagnes-Le Cros's form was patchy. They were stolidly mid-table and could have done with in-form Sam Alexander: he'd left in the transfer window. He'd scored a goal a game since joining Espaly FC in Espaly-Saint-Marcel in south-central France.

Back in England, QPR's good season had petered out with a poor run of form from late March to the end of April, guaranteeing mid-table anonymity. I was delighted for my second team, Exeter City. After years of knocking on the door of promotion to League One, they finally made it on 26 April with a 2-1 win over Barrow at St James Park. That had to be good news for Sonny Cox. He'd done well on loan at Weston-Super-Mare, notching up invaluable experience. I was sure he'd be ready to step into League One. As for the big fella, John was quietly excited – Liverpool had won the FA Cup final the previous day, were on form and in with a genuine chance of winning the quadruple of EFL Cup, FA Cup, Premier League and European Champions League. I hoped Liverpool would pull it off, too, and was delighted by some news closer to home that John gave me: on Saturday, Spezia Calcio won 3-2 away to Udinese. The result meant they were safe. Poor Genoa were in the mire. A total of 13 managerial changes in the past five years and a pitiful four wins for the season were not a recipe for success. Today, they had to win at Napoli, an impossible task. Sampdoria were also safe. I wondered if their fans would march through the streets of Genoa, with a coffin draped in the colours of their sworn foes, as and when *Il Grifone* were relegated.

For now, a humble game in the sixth tier of French football was what mattered. It was an intriguing match for one simple reason: seeing Carnoux play would mean PSG weren't the only champions I saw live over the 2021/22 season.

Carnoux, from the commune of Carnoux-de-Provence ten miles south-east of Marseille, were head and shoulders above Cagnes-Le Cros. The differential wasn't as pronounced as the Nice v Versailles clash, but the two clubs were functioning at different levels. Where *Les Cagnois* were sluggish and slow to react, Carnoux were quick and incisive. Where Cagnes were clueless, Carnoux had ideas and options. And while Cagnes-Le Cros's players weren't poor, they wanted for cohesion. In contrast, those in the all-blue kit of Carnoux had the edge when it came to skill – and they played together as a unit.

The final score was Cagnes-Le Cros 2 Carnoux 4. John and I couldn't work out how Cagnes got on the scoresheet – and why Carnoux only scored four. Perhaps we were a little distracted. One of the most exciting Premier League seasons in years was heading to its denouement. Manchester City were away to West Ham. Defeat would put Liverpool in the driving seat. Incredibly, West Ham were 2-0 up at half-time, only for City to claw their way back to a 2-2 draw. John and I spent a fair bit of time checking the score on our phones rather than watching the game. We weren't alone. A lot of the Frenchmen around us were also glued to how the Premier League title race was unfolding.

It was the final game we'd record together for the podcast. As ever, it had been a great afternoon. It was warm and sunny. The clubhouse sold chilled lager. No one objected when we took a couple of cans into the stand. We sat behind some typically noisy locals, who were drinking too. With six goals, and even allowing for spells of Premier League distraction, it was an entertaining game. Carnoux would go on to be crowned deserved champions of Regional 1.

Afterwards, as we drove back to Menton, John asked me if the plan was still to return to England at the end of the summer. It's fair to say he felt we'd be better off staying on the Med.

'I mean, a day like we've just had. Come on!'

It wasn't just the trip to Cagnes-sur-Mer that had gone so well. I'd now recovered my fitness and was holding my own in our games of five-a-side. We'd played that morning. Everything else about Menton was the same – and getting better.

'Yes, it is,' I replied. 'We complete on the house sale in a couple of weeks. We should be in the Wiltshire house by August.'

'That's a bit tight, isn't it?' said John.

It was. But there was no time to think. I'd got hold of two tickets for AEK Athens v Olympiacos. It was the only game in Athens I could get to all season. It was in two days' time, and I was flying to Athens from Nice airport the next day.

14

May 2022

To Athens, for Stan

IT'S JUST like the night before my first QPR game,
all those years ago, at Bristol City. I'm so excited I can't
sleep. This is absurd. I'm a grown man of 56. It's annoying.
Very annoying. Work has been relentless. I need my sleep.
Maybe work is why I'm so restive. Tomorrow I'm to give
evidence to a Ministry of Justice commission on Strategic
Lawsuits Against Public Participation (SLAPPs).
Remotely, via video link, from my room in the Hotel
Acropolis View in Athens. I've spent the flight from Nice
to Athens reading up on everything, most of the evening,
too. But I haven't done anything like this before. I'm
nervous. I believe in freedom of expression. I loathe the
way in which the UK's libel laws are exploited by the rich
and unscrupulous to kill off stories of huge importance
to the public. But tomorrow's session isn't my standard
working fare.

Moving out of my comfort zone isn't helped by the
surreal setting from which I'll be contributing. There,

no more than a ten-minute walk to the west, is the Acropolis and its temple, the Parthenon. I'd walked around the surprisingly tranquil ancient hill almost as soon as I'd checked in. Good old Greece, the birthplace of democracy. What would Pericles, first citizen of Athens and godfather of Athenian democracy, make of SLAPPs? An intimidatory lawsuit brought not because the claimant believes he, she or, often enough, it (companies are great friends of SLAPPs) has been meaningfully defamed but as a tactical move to silence criticism. Pericles would have treated a SLAPP and those who use them with the contempt they deserve. But noble thoughts are juxtaposed by more earthy ones, given my hotel's location. It's a former, perhaps still, red light district. There's a strip bar on the corner opposite and, next to the hotel, a sex shop.

I doze off. Fitful sleep. Thoughts of work keep intruding. I wake up and have breakfast, the Acropolis across the way. I go back to my room and do some more reading. I start to warm to the task. Journalism hasn't always got it right. No one could defend the practice of phone hacking or the times when bearing witness to the truth goes AWOL, the press collectively adopting an agenda and forgetting the basics, as, for example, in the reporting of the murder of Joanna Yates. But journalism is important. It's vital. Without journalism, we may as well accept the post-truth nonsense of Donald Trump, the brazen lies of the Brexiteers, the disgusting fabrications of Alex Jones. Without journalism, we can give Vladimir Putin a pass and ignore Russia's invasion of Ukraine.

And yet week in, week out, the UK press receive letters threatening all manner of legally inflicted oblivion, if enquiries persist into a given individual's activities or if an editor has the temerity to publish a story. The letters are identikit. They drip with pomposity and aggression. I often wonder what it's like to work on that side of the legal fence. To wake up and start your day knowing that you will later send a letter or email full of bluster and self-importance, nit-picking, petty, mean-spirited and about as far removed from any ideal of justice as possible. A letter that demands compliance – or else! A letter that routinely insults its recipient, that laments their sloppy journalism or pathetic failure to understand the law, that bilks the system. What's it like to look in the mirror and say, 'That's my job. Today I will go forth and spew some bile'?

The morning wears on. I look forward to saying my bit. The session begins at what is 4pm in Athens. It goes well. There's a fair following wind back in the UK. Perhaps the government will do something about SLAPPs.

The moment it's over, I change out of my smart white shirt and jacket, put on something casual and bolt for the door. Because now, at last, it's time to go to AEK Athens v Olympiacos.

* * *

I didn't think I'd make it to Athens. Life was jam-packed with a thousand different commitments. How would I ever cram it in? But while waiting for a flight from Heathrow to Nice on one of the trips back home in early May, I'd looked up AEK's fixtures. The Super League in Greece had entered its play-off phase. Olympiacos, from the Piraeus port area of Athens, were already the winners. They'd come top of the regular season, which consists of

14 teams playing each other from August to May. There's then a play-off among the top six teams to determine the champions. Olympiacos were dead certs, and duly delivered. But the most successful club in Greek history (47 league titles, 28 cups, four super cups, and counting) had a couple of games left before their players could put their feet up. One of them was away to AEK Athens on the evening of Tuesday, 17 May.

I dropped a line to a friend who lives in Athens, Paola Menachem. Paola is an AEK fan. She said she'd love to go the game and would get two tickets for the Olympic Stadium.

Wait – the Olympic Stadium? That's not where QPR played, just over 45 years ago. The UEFA Cup quarter-final was played at AEK's Nikos Goumas Stadium in the Nea Filadelfeia suburb in north-west Athens. Had AEK moved away?

I had Stan's autobiography with me. I turned to the section on the AEK away game. The book didn't seem to name the stadium in which the match was played. But I know my QPR facts (some of them, at least). I was certain the game was played at the Nikos Goumas stadium. I read on, searching in vain for a namecheck. Instead, I met a vision of Mediterranean football that although I'd once read, I'd forgotten. This was no sun-kissed idyll, no Tika-taka between the stands followed by souvlaki, raki and, next day, some downtime by the beach. Stan and QPR were confronted by a capacity crowd of 35,000, whose hostility wasn't merely verbal. They threw apples onto the pitch before the game, and then, as the QPR players disembarked from the team coach and walked through a narrow entrance by one of the stands, urinated on them.

With three key players for QPR missing – Gerry Francis, Dave Thomas and Dave Clement – the night didn't go the Rs' way. AEK scored three, to take the game level on aggregate. Bowles had a torrid time. He quips he had to time his forays down the wing so he could deploy the linesman 'as a human shield' – because of the onslaught of apples hurled at him by AEK's fans. When they ran out of apples, they started using tomatoes. Stan approved: *'After you've had big hard apples chucked at you for a full fifteen minutes, it makes for quite a pleasant change to have squishy tomatoes hit you.'* More seriously, it seems the crowd's anger may have affected the referee. Certainly, Stan felt 50-50 decisions went against QPR, and he quotes Frank McLintock, one of QPR's centre-halves, on the ferocity of AEK's fans.

'The Greek fans were unbelievable during the game. They were really, really worked up – well over the top. One of them kicked his foot through the back of the dug-out where Dave Sexton and the others were sitting. It was real hysteria. I think there might have been a riot if we had won.'

In another of *Stan the Man's* great lines, Stan has the pitch at full-time at Nikos Goumas resembling 'a bountiful orchard without the trees'. The final score was 7-6 on penalties to AEK. Peter Eastoe and Dave Webb were the two QPR players who failed to score from the spot. No one could blame them. Stan didn't. His portrait of the bountiful orchard without any trees is one accompanied by ever-present danger and incipient catastrophe, the home fans baying for blood and on the brink of drawing it. So much for etymology: Nea Filadelfeia means 'New Philadelphia' and is derived from the Ancient Greek word *phílos* (φίλος), meaning 'love', and *adelphós* (ἀδελφός), meaning 'brother'. Put them together and even one of the worst Ancient Greek A-level students England has seen can tell you the word means 'brotherly love'. It was nowhere to be seen that night in Athens. How do you keep your nerve and take a penalty in an environment like that? Stan, of course, did, blithely scoring the first QPR kick as if he was in a training session in front of the Loft. That was one of the things about Stan Bowles. His courage. He wasn't afraid of anything.

I checked elsewhere. AEK departed the Nikos Goumas Stadium in 2003. By then, it had seen better days, but the Athens earthquake in 1999 (which killed 143 people and caused damage to more than 100 buildings at an estimated cost of $3bn to $4.2bn) pushed it from relic to health hazard. AEK had to move. Their last game at the Nikos Goumas was a 4-0 win against Aris on 3 May 2003. Luckily for AEK, they only had the summer to wait for the Athens Olympics 2004 to be over – whereupon they moved into the Olympic Stadium in the Maroussi district.

* * *

Paola was intrigued by my fidelity to QPR and Stan Bowles.

'They're not a big team, are they?' she asked, as she drove us from her house in Maroussi to the Olympic Stadium. 'And this Stan Bowles, I don't think I've heard of him. You've come here for him? Who is he?'

Paola is a lawyer. She's an exceptionally bright woman, whose English is perfect. She's fluent in other languages, too. I could have embarked on a lengthy eulogy about Bowles, and she'd have understood it completely. But at that point, there we were, haggling with an official about where to park the car. Not in the stadium car park, it turned out. The official was adamant. Most insistent, waving us away – even though the vast car park had virtually nothing in it with not long to go before kick-off. We found a spot outside and made our way to the entrance.

I hadn't answered Paola's question. Lawyers don't tend to forget things and she asked again a little later, once we'd found our seats. I began to say something about heroes, and was going to add Alzheimer's disease, and the renaming of the Ellerslie Road stand as the Stanley Bowles Stand, and the enduring effect Bowles had had upon me, ever since I first saw him play at Bristol City a few days after defeat to AEK, nearly half a century ago, but AEK's ultras had started to arrive.

If elsewhere on the Med, along the Italian and French Rivieras at least, I'd concluded that most of what the ultras got up to was mere posturing, AEK's hardcore didn't look like they were mucking about. Before they arrived, the stadium had been all but empty. Both it and the pre-match ambience felt tired. Worn-down, like an old dog forcing itself through the motions, desperate only to lie down and sleep. The Olympic Stadium holds just under 70,000 people. With 20 minutes until kick-off, only about 500 people had turned up. Then the AEK diehards swarmed in through the north-west turnstiles, filling the end behind the goal. There must have been about 2,000 of them. They were not in a good mood. Their shouting and drumming was accompanied by bottle after bottle being thrown over high netting and on to the athletics track. For a split second, two thoughts went through my mind: one, these guys must be javelin throwers in their spare time (their reach was phenomenal) and, two, the pitch at the Nikos Goumas, from photographs I'd seen, was only a couple of yards from the stands. It would have been easy to pelt QPR's players with apples and tomatoes and whatever else was to hand.

The noises mutated into boos, whistles and catcalls when AEK's team was read out over the tannoy. I'd never heard anything like it. The home fans were enraged by their own side. They were apoplectic. A large banner was unfurled, whose words Paola translated:

'It says, "fucking players, fucking managers, AEK never dies". Then it tells the owners to wake up and go. They don't like the current owners.'

The display of enmity grew. Half the AEK ultras were bare-chested, half kept their mainly black shirts and T-shirts on. It was hot in Athens, but the display of flesh wasn't just down to the heat. It was a display of naked passion, of the purity of their support, something that had struck a chord with the founder of Marseille's MTP ultras, Patrice de Péretti. Otherwise known as Depé, Péretti watched a Marseille v AEK game in 1989 when he was a teenager. AEK's fans numbered 100 or so. Depé was astonished to see them bellowing their support, bare-chested, throughout the game, matching the clamour of *Les Marseillais*. He vowed he'd do the same for his club, spawning *Marseille Trop Puissant* (Marseille, All Powerful), the MTP ultras. They did the same, following their *capo* even at away games when it was -12°C and stripping to the waist. Depé had died young of a burst aneurysm in 2000. By then, he was a legend in Marseille.

Links between Marseille and AEK's ultras continue to this day, but while Marseille's pogoing fans had dominated the Stade Louis II, barbarity was at bay. It isn't always – Nice v Marseille was enough recent proof of the madness that lurks – but there was no sense at the Monaco game that anyone might come to grief.

Not so at the Olympic Stadium, as the game headed for kick-off. AEK's supporters looked and sounded ready to kill.

They sustained their fury even when AEK Athens took the lead through Swiss winger Steven Zuber. It was a decent goal, too – a well-hit, right-footed drive from outside the area. AEK had looked the livelier of the two sides and were rightly ahead thanks to a goal of some quality. Their fans just kept booing. Paola translated one of the chants, 'They're saying the owner is a fucking big dick.'

Paola also told me that tonight's game would be the last AEK Athens would play in the Olympic Stadium. 'They're going home, back to Nea Filadelfeia. The new stadium is on the site of the old Nikos Goumas Stadium. They're training an eagle to fly from corner to corner before each game.'

Was this a crowd-pleaser inspired by OGC Nice's Mèfi the eagle? Probably not. Paola pointed out AEK's emblem, a double-headed eagle, and explained both its background and AEK's colours of black and gold. 'AEK stands for Athletic Union of Constantinople,' she said. 'AEK's colours represent the club's links with Constantinople, which was part of Greece until it was conquered by the Turks in 1453. The eagle and the colours are a reminder of the Byzantine Empire, of the people from Constantinople in Greece.'

Paola said AEK's new stadium, the Agia Sophia Stadium, would be ready by the summer. It would house 32,000 fans and had an underground road system by which the teams would arrive.

Anything that kept players and officials apart from AEK's fans seemed wise. Even being a goal up did nothing to quell their rage. They were so incensed I wondered if they'd be happy when Moroccan international striker, Al Arabi, nodded home for Olympiacos after a flowing move on the left wing. No. The equaliser was met by a cascade of bottles.

Both sides' players seemed immune to the antics of the crowd. Fortunately, a decent game of football was happening, with Pierre Kunde, the Olympiacos number eight and a central midfielder for Cameroon, impressing, likewise Levi García, up front for AEK and a member of the Trinidad and Tobago national side. Both were strong and clever and good on the ball. García's hard work paid off soon after the interval when he nimbly held his line and then leapt high above a defender to head the ball into the net. It was a goal Les Ferdinand, much-loved at QPR and known for his prodigious leaps, would have been proud of.

Cue at least a half-hearted cheer? Just about. But AEK's fans, who had spent the entire first half on their feet, drumming, shouting abuse and throwing bottles, now chose to sit down. For the most part, they said and did nothing. Were they spent, exhausted after having vented so much anger? I don't think so. I think the display of indifference was another form of protest. Paola was relieved. 'So much of what they say is about women, the players' mothers, their wives, their girlfriends,' she said. 'It's really horrible. They hate women. I messaged my girlfriends about this at half-time, but they just say I'm naïve. They say this is normal for a football match.'

The relative repose was welcome, but still, when Zuber was put through to score his second, only for the goal to be disallowed for offside, a few of the faithful took this as insult enough to justify the throwing of a few more missiles over the net and on to the track. Likewise, when Al Arabi bagged his second in the 69th minute. It was a soft goal. AEK gave the ball away in their own half and failed to muster any commitment to quell the resulting Olympiacos attack. The ball bounced on to Al Arabi's chest and he smashed it in from a distance of one foot. There was a whiff of offside in the build-up, but the goal stood. AEK weren't so lucky when they then scored from a free kick. A VAR review confirmed this was another goal that would be chalked off for offside.

The game looked set for a 2-2 draw. As it neared the end, AEK's fans were back on their feet, drumming and chanting. Bottle after bottle came raining down on to the track. Riot police mustered, hands on holsters. In the 87th minute, Al Arabi was there again, picking up the scraps and first to react to a loose ball inside the six-yard box; 3-2 to Olympiacos. Another flurry of bottles flew over the net.

The AEK ultras had an endless supply. Where on earth did they get them?

The game ended in a 3-2 win for Olympiacos. A draw would have been fair. For all the ire of their fans, AEK weren't a bad side. They'd been a little unlucky on the night and were guilty of some slack defending, but passed the ball well and were good going forward. The AEK hardcore didn't share this view. One of them made his way on to the track and used a flare to set alight each letter in the long banner hung on the lowest part of the stand that said AEK never dies and called for the owners to go. The police stood and watched. Bottles kept coming. Paola and I decided to leave.

* * *

Paola and I went for dinner in central Athens after the game. The Greeks have a tradition of being hospitable to foreigners (a tradition they seem to forget when it comes to football), and Paola exemplified it, expertly manoeuvring her car in and out of the city's narrow streets to point out sight after sight, insisting we stop at the Panathenaic Stadium (the only stadium in the world made entirely of marble, a glorious sight and still the finishing point for the Athens marathon), taking me to the Thanasis restaurant (a buzzing place in a square in Monastiraki, where we ate wonderful souvlaki), and then meandering through the streets, taking in the hubbub of this chaotic city, a place that had the edge over Genoa when it came to beautiful confusion. We hadn't seen each other for many years, and talked so much that we both forgot about Paola's question at the beginning of the night: why Stan Bowles?

Around midnight, Paola dropped me off at the Acropolis View. Among the goodbyes she said, 'You'll have to come back and see AEK in the new stadium.'

Afterwards, I sat at the tiny desk in my hotel room and went over the day's events. Breakfast, work, a walk to stretch my legs, more work and then giving evidence to the Ministry of Justice commission on SLAPPs, from this same desk. Racing straight afterwards in a taxi to Paola's house in Maroussi. Having a Greek woman start talking to me in the street outside, as I wondered if I was in the right place. She turned out to be Paola's mother. Along came Paola with one of her daughters. Off we went to the Olympic Stadium. Watching the game, watching the fans, seeing some sights, going for dinner and now here I was, my mission accomplished. I'd had a season on the Med and I'd made it to Athens.

But why Stan Bowles? And why had I come all the way to Athens?

I looked up a piece I'd written for *The Times Literary Supplement*, about the threads linking the American writer Robert Coover, myself and Bowles. I'd pitched the idea to James Campbell, then the author of the *TLS*'s Notebook column and editor of its Freelance section. He'd said yes and the piece ran in the *TLS* of 17 April 2015. If I sent it to Paola, would it have the answers?

> In the mid-1990s, I was in my 20s, working as a libel lawyer in London. On Saturday afternoons, I supported the Shepherd's Bush-based football club Queens Park Rangers, and, when they were playing away from home, I turned out

for a Saturday league team in Kent. My fellow
striker's father was Tono Masoliver, a Spanish
poet who knew the American writer Robert
Coover. I had written a novel and was desperate
to escape a caseload that involved a strange and
mercurial partner and taking witness statements
from the beleaguered politician Neil Hamilton
and his formidable wife Christine. Tono passed
on Coover's address at Brown University,
Rhode Island, saying he might take a look at my
manuscript. We had, apparently, something in
common: we were both QPR fans.

I'd studied Coover at university, and knew
him as an American postmodernist who came
to prominence in the 1960s along with Donald
Barthelme, John Barth and Saul Bellow. His first
novel, *The Origin of the Brunists*, won the 1966
William Faulkner Award. *Pricksongs and Descants*
was published three years later. Its concluding
story 'The Hat Act' is about a failing magician.
The stage directions included in the text –
'Applause', 'Whistling and shouting', developing
into 'Screams of terror', 'Weeping' – were not
inspired by QPR.

Coover's response to the pages I sent him
arrived in July 1994, 'Normally, I don't respond
to requests for manuscript critiques (I get one
a week or so – I'd do nothing else), but a QPR
supporter, being rare as a Panda, deserves at
least a reply.' The letter went on to find some
good, some bad, in a chaotic effort that, despite

Coover's kind description of it as 'well-written, often clever, probably publishable', deserves the literary oblivion it has achieved.

A year later, on 3 May 1995, Coover and I went to Upton Park in east London to watch QPR play West Ham United. It was an evening game. I was still plying my trade as a libel lawyer, without much professional or personal satisfaction. My diary entry for that day reads, 'Work was a little better since I felt optimistic about meeting Robert Coover. He was craggy, interesting and as devoted to QPR as I am.' With us for a match that resulted in a 0-0 draw was David Wingrove, the author of some science-fiction novels. Coover introduced me to Wingrove as 'a writer', something that at once jarred and touched me: I wasn't a writer. I was a libel lawyer. Writing for a living – proper writing, not penning letters threatening legal action – felt a long way off.

That night, we talked little of writing and much of Queens Park Rangers. Supporting the team does not yield much by way of pleasure, but the club has a tradition, of sorts, which Coover, I and other devotees adore: many great number tens – the magicians of football – have worn the blue and white hoops. My favourite is Stan Bowles, who could do anything with a football, and was just as adept at filling out betting slips.

After that, I fell out of touch with Coover. He spent most of his time from the mid-1990s on at Brown, working as a professor and writing. During the same period, QPR sank from the leading division to the second and then the third. Meanwhile, I was sacked from a law firm for being what is euphemistically called 'tired and emotional'. Dark days in a Wandsworth bedsit led to a decline in alcohol consumption and reinvention as a sports writer. I wrote about Bowles and covered matches, but once a lawyer (even an errant one), always a lawyer, and so I did a bit of libel on the side. Throughout everything, I went to watch QPR.

In 2012, Keith Carabine, then the chairman of the Joseph Conrad Society, read a book I wrote about boxing, *Wrecking Machine*. Its epigraph is taken from Lord Jim. 'In the destructive element immerse,' Stein says to Marlow. Keith wrote me a letter, but discussion of Conrad was soon replaced by that of football. A Manchester City fan, Keith was intrigued to learn of my fidelity to QPR. 'I was in Jamaica in the 1970s and met the Rangers team on a pre-season tour there,' he said. 'What a side. Phil Parkes, Gerry Francis and the wizard himself – Stan Bowles. I introduced some of them to the American writer Robert Coover. He became a passionate QPR fan.'

Extraordinary! I told him about going with Coover to West Ham vs QPR all those years ago, and of his generosity in reading my manuscript. Keith said that Coover was coming to London. And so, at the beginning of October 2013, thanks to Keith, Coover and I met for the second time to watch QPR – again for a match against West Ham, though this time at the team's Loftus Road Stadium in Shepherd's Bush.

In the nearby Vine Leaves Taverna, we discussed the team's disastrous form. With us was Coover's wife, Pilar and Tono's son, Yashin, a West Ham fan. Yashin thought his team would edge it. Keith thought it would be a draw. Because hope springs more eternal among the Loftus Road faithful than other fans, Coover and I predicted we'd sneak a win. At half-time, QPR were so bad, I felt embarrassed. We lost 2–1. Relegation came at the end of the season.

It's February of this year and Coover and I are in the Vine Leaves Taverna once again. It's his favourite pre-match haunt, the place he and Pilar would visit before games when they lived in London. They're back, renting a place in Belsize Park. Coover tells me he comes to London to write. 'Even though I've retired from Brown, I live very close to the place. I never get a moment's peace.' The bonus of being here – and a curious bonus it can be – is that he is able to see QPR regularly. He tells me that at Brown he and his son, Rod, flew the Rangers flag, and that they were not alone – there's another professor who's a QPR fan. He's still plagued by would-be writers asking for critiques. He does his best to help, but it's hard. 'It's a very tough business these days.'

Aged 83, he himself is as prolific as ever. Last year, he published *The Brunist Day of Wrath*, a sequel to *The Origin of the Brunists*. It's about a cult, the Brunist sect, for whom Rapture is a fact of life.

I mention that I've written a couple of novels since we first met. 'The third might just be OK,' I say, but quickly add, 'Please don't worry – this isn't a request for a critique.' Coover meets this statement inscrutably. We finish our lunch at the Vine Leaves and meander along the streets of Shepherd's Bush to watch QPR play Manchester United. The first half is even and we exchange words of hope, but our dreams are dashed. United finish as 2-0 winners. Coover and I shuffle out with the faithful, into the darkness, he to catch the Tube to Belsize Park, me to drive west to my home in Cornwall, our fate as participants in the cult of QPR as devoid of rapture as ever. I think of life's strange threads and I think about Coover, a writer who plays with fables, who can dazzle in a single sentence, and I think of QPR's magical number ten, my beloved Stan Bowles.

That was a large part of it. Magic. But the magic of Stanley Bowles went beyond what he could do with a football.

I'd often ask myself, as I got older, whether it was a good thing that a gambling addict with a wandering eye, who liked a drink or five, was my role model. As both a pre-pubescent child and teenager, I'd idolised Bowles. I'd learnt to do trick after trick with a football. I once managed

1,376 keepie-ups in a row. What good had it done me? I'd
only ever been an average amateur player. And did the
1980s and '90s wrongly glamorise the likes of Bowles,
anyway? There were newspaper and magazine articles and
books aplenty on the entertainers of Bowles's era, chief
among them Rob Steen's *The Mavericks: When English
Football Wore Flares.* First published in 1995, I loved Steen's
book, a celebration of individualism in the form of players
such as Bowles, Rodney Marsh, Frank Worthington and
Charlie George. Tony Currie was included too, meaning
that QPR could boast three of Steen's total of seven
mavericks. I was proud of that, but should I have been?
QPR hadn't exactly dominated English football. A lot of
other clubs are much more successful. And isn't life about
community, about conventions and norms and adhering
to codes spoken or unspoken, not self-determination and
the belief that the rules don't apply?

Certainly, my own life hadn't been a textbook of linear
progress. I'd had my own demons. I couldn't say I was any
more of a role model than Stan.

Bowles's family announced he'd been diagnosed with
Alzheimer's disease in June 2015. Three years later, *The
Mirror* ran a story that dubbed Bowles 'the Lionel Messi
of the '70s', in which Bowles's great friend Don Shanks
revealed that the disease had progressed to the extent that
the former player no longer knew who he was. QPR held
a 'Stan Bowles Day' and Shanks himself ran the New
York Marathon in four hours and 11 minutes to raise
£30,000 for his friend and the Alzheimer's Society. Over
the course of the 2021/22 season, QPR set about renaming
the Ellerslie Road Stand. It would become the Stanley

Bowles Stand, to be officially opened at the start of the 2022/23 campaign.

I lay down to go to sleep in my room in the Hotel Acropolis View. At the beginning of this season on the Med, I'd put Athens in my sights more by way of a whim than a definite plan. Early on, I'd realised any conflation of my love of the Med with one my hero might have had was a delusion. But Stan was still a hero. He always would be.

I'd come to Athens to pay homage to a man I'd never meet, to a club that would never be a Liverpool or Manchester City. To Bowles, for his honesty. The courage to be only ever himself. To QPR, because of *La força d'un sentiment*.

Before I fell asleep, the image of a lost Stan Bowles swirled in my mind. A man in his 70s not knowing where he is, clinging to his family and Shanks for support. How cruel fate can be.

Then I thought of Bowles running down the wing at the Nikos Goumas Stadium when QPR played AEK Athens 45 years ago, enjoying the feel of a squishy tomato rather than an apple. I smiled and slept the deepest sleep I'd had for years.

15

May 2022

Possibly the Best Football Patch in the World

THE BELL on the old church in the centre of the village tolls. It's 4pm on Saturday, 29 May. I take a football out of my rucksack and, standing on the edge of the pitch, kick it towards the goal at the far end. Next to the goal, there's a concrete wall. It's a little wider than the goal. On the wall, which is a fraction lower than the goal, is a single word. The first two letters are in yellow. The third is in light orange. One half of the fourth letter, an M, is in red, the other is blue. Darkening shades of blue, to near-black, complete the final three letters.

BRUMANO

I jog slowly to the ball. The pitch is about half to two-thirds the size of a full 11-a-side pitch. I'm not dressed for football. But when I reach the ball I strike it into the net. I run and retrieve it, and then run as if I'm dribbling the ball to the goal at the other end. I side-foot the ball into the goal. I run back to the other end. As I approach the

Brumano wall, there are old doors on a concrete outhouse on my left. One says 'Locali', the other 'Ospiti'. One for locals, one for guests. One for the home players, one for the away side. I do some keepie-ups. I hit the ball against the concrete wall, control it and volley it back against the wall again. I keep doing this until my 56-year-old legs begin to protest.

There is no one in the park, which is called Parco Giochi. It has two children's play areas at the end opposite the Brumano wall. There's a clubhouse along the eastern side of the pitch. On the western, village, side, there's some terracing. Perhaps 50 people could gather there. All around are the high hills and green trees and distant mountains of Lombardy. There is no one here. Brumano's population is now no more than 100. The only sound is birdsong.

A couple in their 60s walk along the road above the park. They look at me. *Why is that middle-aged man kicking a football in Parco Giochi? On his own?*

Eventually, I tire. I sit down on a wooden bench in front of the clubhouse. I stare at the pitch, and, staring back into the past, I can remember the walk – left out of Cristina's family's apartment, along the road for a bit, take a right down a short incline, and then I was here, at the park, to play football all day long, every day for three weeks.

Calcio.

The best three weeks of my life.

* * *

We'd arrived in Brumano the previous day. I did a poor job of trying to hide my excitement as we wended our way up the mountain roads. I felt elated in a way I couldn't explain. I was also worried that, if I tried to explain it, I might choke up. 'It's OK,' said Caroline. 'It's OK to be excited.'

We stopped the car at the sign for the village, 'Brumano – Foresta del Resegone'. I got out and touched the sign. I couldn't believe we were here, that I'd finally come back to Brumano.

We drove on the short distance into the village. At once, I recognised Cristina's family's place. I slowed the car. Yes, there it was, on the left. It looked empty. In one of the flats above, a woman appeared in a window. We drove on, slowly. Instinctively I took the first right. It took us down to Parco Giochi. It was exactly as I remembered. A tear came to my eye. Back after 40 years. Caroline walked the dogs around the park, while I took Maud to the play area. We agreed I'd return on my own the next day.

On the drive to the neighbouring village of Fuipiano Valle Imagna, Maud chattered away. I couldn't get a word out to tell Caroline what I felt. We managed to talk properly earlier on the journey from Menton, though, when Maud had a nap. We grappled with something that was troubling both of us: we were set for a much longer delay than we'd anticipated in the purchase of the house in Wiltshire. The issues with the estate were protracted; to say progress was glacial would be an exaggeration. There was a corollary. Because, with our house in Cornwall about to be sold, we would soon neither have a UK address nor be about to acquire one, we would struggle to enrol Maud in the school we'd found, just a mile from the house in Wiltshire. And then, because we probably wouldn't own the house until the end of the year, or possibly not until early 2023, would it be right to pluck Maud out of the final year of *maternelle*, mid-stream?

Should we bite the bullet and stay in France for another year? If we did, Maud would complete three consecutive years at École Adrien Camaret. It was a lovely school and, with three years rather than two in France, she would probably retain her French. We'd all be settled as a family and could plan our new life in Wiltshire properly.

We decided to stay in France.

The next day, Stefan, the amiable and laconic owner of the Hotel Ristorante Moderno in Fuipiano, lent me a bike. Caroline and Maud stayed put, to enjoy the hotel's spa. It's a short but hard ride, with a lot of steep hills, but I loved every minute of it. And I loved being back on the football pitch in the village of Brumano, kicking a ball around, as if, for a few minutes, I was as free of responsibility as the 16-year-old who'd been here 40 years ago.

Afterwards, sitting on the wooden bench, I looked around, at the village, the dense green of the trees on the mountains, one or two ridges away in the distance, and back down to the football pitch at my feet. Brumano had lurked in my mind since the day I left the place. I'd always wanted to come back, and I think I would have done one day, but probably a good few years later, an odyssey to keep me occupied in retirement. But I'd done it. I was here on a warm, late-spring day. The grass was as deep-green as ever. I hadn't invented the beauty; it wasn't a trick of my memory. This barely known pocket of Italy may as well be heaven.

Suddenly, I felt sad. Empty in a way I hadn't known before. I looked to try and find my 16-year-old self, running up and down the pitch, the boy who only wanted to play football and had a hero called Stan Bowles. The boy with not a care in the world. The boy with his life ahead of him, a life that had had all manner of twists and turns and happiness and disasters.

The boy was there, for a second, but I couldn't catch hold of him. He was too quick, if I'd seen him at all. Had I? Now only a faint outline remained, an ungraspable chiaroscuro. The boy was gone. Stan Bowles was gone, too – at least, the Stan I and so many others had adored, the Stan whose flicks and tricks I'd tried out on the local Italian lads here, all those years ago. What existed, now? It was all gone. It would never come back.

I tried to make sense of how I'd got here. I'd decided to write about Mediterranean football along the Italian and French Rivieras. I'd moved to Menton because of a family road trip more than 40 years ago. Back then, as a 15-year-old, I'd met a girl called Cristina. Things hadn't worked out with her in England, but it'd been arranged that I'd still come and stay with her family in Italy. I did, a year later, when I was 16. Turned out they had a place in Brumano. Did they still, I wondered?

I packed the ball away and cycled into the village. There was a bar I used to go to; I'd noticed it as we drove through the day before. The Bar Caffé Persech was open and doing a roaring trade. I felt shy but pushed the door open. A blonde woman was behind the counter. She was about my age. She wasn't Cristina, but I'd got friendly with a girl called Raffaella all those years ago. We used to talk in the bar. Raffaella was always there. Was this the family business, and was this woman Raffaella?

I ordered a coffee and a glass of water. I asked the woman if she spoke English. She did not, but she went outside and returned with an Italian man who did, albeit imperfectly. I asked if the woman knew Cristina's family and told her the surname. Initially, she looked blank. But then, yes, she remembered. They used to have an apartment as you arrived in the village. And then they sold it and bought a different one, up above the church. But, about eight years ago (she thought but was not sure), the family sold it. The woman hadn't seen them since.

Why, though, did I want to know? I didn't mention *calcio*. I told my translator and the woman behind the counter of having stayed here, 40 years ago, with Cristina's family.

Ah, they said. But sorry. They're not here anymore. Very sorry. Very, very sorry.

Adding 'Are you Raffaella?' would have sounded odd after this. I didn't ask. Blushing, as if once again I was 16 and awkward, I paid for my coffee and left.

The next day, a light rain was falling. I felt sorry for John. The night before, Liverpool had lost 1-0 to Real Madrid in the Champions League Final. I'd watched the game in what I think is Fuipiano's only bar with four Danes, who were on a hiking holiday. We packed up and left Fuipiano, taking the twisty mountain road to Brumano. The Bar Caffé Persech was closed. Even if I'd plucked up the courage, this trip would not see me asking the woman if she was Raffaella.

We drove to the Parco Giochi, parking the car on the road above the park. The rain had begun to fall more heavily. Caroline and I looked at each other. Should we?

We smiled. I turned to Maud, sitting in her child seat in the back.

'Maudy?' I said.

'Yes, Daddy?'

'Do you want to play football on a football patch?' I asked.

'Yes, Daddy!'

And Maud and I kicked the ball back and forth on the football pitch in the village of Brumano.

The Games

August 2021

7 August – Exeter City 0 Bradford City 0 (League Two)

24 August – Queens Park Rangers 2 Oxford United 0 (EFL Cup)

September 2021

11 September – AS Monaco 0 Olympique de Marseille 2 (Ligue 1)

18 September – Genoa 1 Fiorentina 2 (Serie A)

22 September – Imperia 1 Sanremese 2 (Coppa Italia)

October 2021

3 October – Sampdoria 3 Udinese 3 (Serie A)

6 October – Sanremese 1 Casale 2 (Serie D)

17 October – Montpellier 1 Lens 0 (Ligue 1)

24 October – Barcelona 1 Real Madrid 2 (La Liga)

November 2021

7 November – Nice 1 Montpellier 0 (Ligue 1)

21 November – Nîmes 2 QRM 1 (Ligue 2)

25 November – Monaco 2 Real Sociedad 1 (Europa League)

December 2021
4 December – Marseille 1 Brest 2 (Ligue 1)
10 December – Genoa 1 Sampdoria 3 (Serie A)

January 2022
14 January – Nice 2 Nantes 1 (Ligue 1)
23 January – Menton 1 Cagnes-le Cros 1 (Regional 1, Méditerranée)
25 January – Queens Park Rangers 0 Swansea City 0 (Championship)
30 January – Villefrance SJB 0 Rousset Ste Victoire 1 (Regional 1, Méditerranée)

February 2022
5 February – Cannes 5 Villefranche SJB 0 (Regional 1, Méditerranée)
13 February – Espanyol 2 Barcelona 2 (La Liga)

March 2022
2 March – Nice 2 Versailles 0 (Coupe de France)
5 March – Nice 1 Paris Saint-Germain 0 (Ligue 1)
19 March – Monaco 3 Paris Saint-Germain 0 (Ligue 1)
30 March – Sanremese 1 Asti 1 (Serie D)

April 2022
3 April – Sampdoria 0 Roma 1 (Serie A)

May 2022
8 May – Spezia 1 Atalanta 3 (Serie A)
15 May – Cagnes-Le Cros 2 Carnoux 4 (Regional 1, Méditerranée)
17 May – AEK Athens 2 Olympiacos 3 (Super League Greece play-offs)

Acknowledgements

My thanks, first, to my own football community. To Doumé and all the players of Foot Five in Menton – thanks for accommodating the immobile Englishman. To Penzance's Five-a-Side Up crew, the Dynamo Choughs and the Thursday Newlyn Non-Athletico guys – the same. Likewise, to Christian and all at London Saturday Soccer. To everyone I've played football with over the years, it's been a joy I couldn't have done without. I hope we can all emulate the great Keith Carabine, both in playing forever and for his generosity of spirit.

In writing this book, I was lucky enough to go to games with John O'Hare and record many episodes of our podcast, *Footy on the Med*. We met some great characters along the way, among them Alex 'The Navigator' Thompson, Eric the charming, handsome Frenchman, Piers the Goalkeeper, Producer Fred, Filmmaker Ed, HammerDonna, Luciano the architect and chef, Paddy the environmental psychologist, Doumé (who is ubiquitous), cycling Stan Bunger (whose feedback on the first draft was much appreciated), Steve the Atlético Medico, Ricardo 'Richard' Ager and Paul

'Young Trafford' Timmis. To everyone who contributed to the podcast, huge thanks and to John, well, what can I say? The biggest fella in Menton has a heart to match. Here's to next season.

Thanks to the fantastic team at Pitch Publishing, especially Jane Camillin, designer Duncan Olner, Gareth Davis, Graham Hales and Dean Rockett. Thanks to Stefan and all at the Hotel Ristorante Moderno in Fuipiano Valle Imagna. Thanks to Paola Menachem for being such a wonderful host in Athens, likewise to Eric and Lydie for their friendship and our trip to Meze, and to Doumé and Ceci for their hospitality and friendship in the hills behind La Turbie.

Talking of Athens – thanks to QPR and to Stan Bowles. Constants in everything. Thanks to Brumano for still being Brumano.

Finally, and most importantly, thanks to everyone in my family: my sons Harry and Elliot, my folks, my brother and sister and their families. Above all, thanks to Caroline and Maud, here with me for these seasons on the Med. Love you.

Bibliography

Bowles, Stan, *The Autobiography* (Orion, 2004)

Donovan, Mike, *Greatest Games – Queens Park Rangers* (Pitch Publishing, 2013)

Hanley, James, *The Closed Harbour* (Oneworld Classics, 2009)

Izzo, Jean-Claude, *Total Chaos* (Editions Gallimard, 1995)

Jones, Ted, *The French Riviera: A Literary Guide for Travellers* (I.B. Tauris & Co, 2004)

Kuper, Simon, *Barça: The Inside Story of the World's Greatest Football Club* (Short Books, 2021)

Macey, Gordon, *Queens Park Rangers: A Complete Record* (Breedon Books, 1993)

McGinniss, Joe, *The Miracle of Castel di Sangro* (Little, Brown, 1999)

Parks, Tim, *A Season with Verona: Travels Around Italy in Search of Illusion, National Character and Goals* (Vintage, 2003)

Parks, Tim, *Italian Ways: On and Off the Rails from Milan to Palermo* (Random House, 2013)

Roden, Cynthia, *Med: A Cookbook* (Ebury Press, 2021)

Rose, Ash, *The QPR Miscellany* (The History Press, 2012)

Steen, Rob, *The Mavericks: When English Football Wore Flares* (Bloomsbury Sport, 1994)

Tossell, David, *All Crazee Now: English Football and Footballers in the 1970s* (Pitch Publishing, 2021)